Twentieth Century English Short Stories

Edited by
Tina Pierce and
Edward Cochrane

LONGMAN

Addison Wesley Longman Limited
Edinburgh Gate, Harlow,
Essex CM20 2JE, England
and Associated Companies throughout the world.

First published by Evans 1979
ISBN 0-17-555850-7
This impression Addison Wesley Longman Ltd. 1996
Fourth impression 1998

Printed in China
SWTC/04

Contents

Acknowledgements

The publishers are grateful to the following for permission to use copyright material in this book:

Laurence Lerner for **Dickon and David** on p. 13; Gerald Duckworth and Co. Ltd. for **The Last Tea** on p. 24 by Dorothy Parker from *The Collected Works of Dorothy Parker* (Duckworth 1973); W. H. Allen and Co. Ltd. for **Enoch's Two Letters** on p. 33 by Alan Sillitoe from *Men, Women and Children;* Laurie Colwin and Chatto and Windus for **Mr Parker** on p. 48 from *Dangerous French Mistress and Other Stories;* Harold Ober Associates Incorporated for **A Member of the Family** on p. 59 from *Voices at Play,* copyright © 1961 by Muriel Spark; John Wain and Curtis Brown Ltd. for **The Valentine Generation** on p. 91 from *Death of the Hind Legs;* Graham Greene, The Bodley Head and William Heinemann for **The Invisible Japanese Gentlemen** on p. 118 from *Collected Stories;* Peter Cowan for **The Tractor** on p. 128; Roald Dahl, Michael Joseph Ltd. and Penguin Books Ltd. for **Parson's Pleasure** on p.146 from *Kiss, Kiss* © 1958 Roald Dahl.

The publishers regret that they have been unable to trace the copyright owners of **Waiting for the Police** by J. Jefferson Farjeon on p. 1, **The Rain Came** by Grace A. Ogot on p. 77, **The Rivals** by Martin Armstrong on p. 107 and would welcome any information on the subject.

Introduction

These short stories and exercises are intended primarily for foreign students who have already done three to four years of English and may be preparing to take the University of Cambridge First Certificate or an equivalent examination. The book will also help students who are not preparing for any specific examination, but who wish to improve their knowledge of English. As the stories have not been abridged or adapted, they may prove useful, too, for British GCSE students.

Writers from Britain, the USA, Australia and Africa, are represented in this collection, our aim being to provide variety of content, style and language. The stories are so arranged that the easier ones are at the beginning of the book.

The exercises have been prepared with the teacher and the classroom in mind. Most of them, however, may also be profitably used for private study. They are intended to increase all-round proficiency in the use of the language and the aim has therefore been to integrate all four of the language learning skills.

Listening Comprehension   These questions have been kept as simple as possible and are based on content. They deal only with small sections of the text, as indicated in each case. The exercises can, of course, also be used as simple Reading Comprehension exercises.

Reading Comprehension   Some of these exercises are based on a set part of the story as indicated; others include questions on the whole of the story requiring simple and straight forward answers. The exercises deal with content, synonyms and antonyms, phraseology and the correct use of prepositions. Practice in sentence construction is also provided.

Discussion and Role-play   The questions and suggestions in these sections are intended to encourage the student to analyse in some detail characters and situations in the text, besides giving consideration to the story as a whole. In some cases we have included topics arising from the story, which should prove useful for general discussion. We have also made suggestions for written work and role-play where appropriate.

Grammar   Two grammar points have been chosen from each story. Although the grammar covered is by no means exhaustive, we have tried to deal with a number of basic points in as varied a way as possible, using the context of the story where suitable.

Words and Phrases   Approximately twenty words and phrases have been selected from each story, their definitions being based on their usage in the context in which they appear. In order that students may become accustomed to using a good monolingual dictionary, we have not included words which are easy to look up. We hope that teachers will encourage discussion of other difficult words or phrases which we have not listed.

The chief purpose of this book is to provide practice in reading, as well as in speaking, writing and listening to English. We hope it will also give pleasure to those who use it, which is why the stories were written in the first place.

Please note that in the questions page numbers and line numbers are referred to as follows: page number, line number. Thus (64, 21) refers to page 64, line 21.

For the Teacher

The use of this collection of stories in the classroom, whether for close study or for extensive reading, will depend largely on the time available. We should like to make the following suggestions:

1 Listening comprehension questions will give the teacher the opportunity of reading out the specified section in the story to test the students' listening skills. Alternatively, the questions can be used as simple tests of reading comprehension.

2 Reading comprehension exercises are most suitable for individual work, in class or at home, after the relevant part of the story has been read. Some of the answers to the exercises may afterwards stimulate useful discussion in the classroom.

3 The discussion and role-play suggestions should not, of course, be attempted until the whole story has been read and is familiar to the students. These suggestions are meant to activate the students to *talk* English as much as possible, so the emphasis here is mainly on *oral* practice. In some cases, it may be a good idea to divide the class into small groups before dealing with the questions in the class as a whole. This should encourage even shy students to put forward their points of view. The teacher should take an active role, just walking round the class listening in, and helping where necessary. At the end of the lesson, one member of each group can report the group's conclusions to the rest of the class. For role-play, working in pairs is usually the most suitable way. Some of the best pairs may like to act in front of the class. This should be fun for the students, and not too much of an ordeal. Correcting of mistakes is best kept as unobtrusive as possible while the students are acting. The teacher can make brief mental notes of the worst mistakes and go through them with the students afterwards.

4 The grammar exercises may be added to as the teacher thinks fit. Where mini-dialogues are included to practise certain structures, the class can be split up into pairs for oral work. This is a good, informal method of helping students to practise their grammar in a more natural context. Some of the exercises can be written down afterwards as extra practice and for reference.

5 The last story, **Parson's Pleasure,** is a good deal longer than the others in this collection. It has been deliberately chosen so that it can be used for individual project work. This may be extended over a period of time – either during term or in the vacation.

We hope that we have provided sufficient variety of exercises for each story, so that teachers can choose those best suited to their classroom needs.

Tina Pierce
Edward Cochrane

Waiting for the Police

J. Jefferson Farjeon

'I wonder where Mr Wainwright's gone?' said Mrs Mayton.

It didn't matter to her in the least where he had gone. All that mattered in regard to her second-floor back was that he paid his three guineas a week regularly for board and lodging, baths extra. But life – and
5   particularly evening life – was notoriously dull in her boarding-house, and every now and again one tried to whip up a little interest.

'Did he go?' asked Monty Smith.

It didn't matter to him, either, but he was as polite as he was pale, and he always did his best to keep any ball rolling.

10   'I thought I heard the front door close,' answered Mrs Mayton.

'Perhaps he went out to post a letter,' suggested Miss Wicks, without pausing in her knitting. She had knitted for seventy years, and looked good for another seventy.

'Or perhaps it wasn't him at all,' added Bella Randall. Bella was the
15   boarding-house lovely, but no one had taken advantage of the fact.

'You mean, it might have been someone else?' inquired Mrs Mayton.

'Yes,' agreed Bella.

They all considered the alternative earnestly. Mr Calthrop, coming suddenly out of a middle-aged doze, joined in the thinking without any
20   idea what he was thinking.

'Perhaps it was Mr Penbury,' said Mrs Mayton, at last. 'He's always popping in and out.'

But it was not Mr Penbury, for that rather eccentric individual walked into the drawing-room a moment later.

25   His arrival interrupted the conversation, and the company reverted to silence. Penbury always had a chilling effect. He possessed a brain, and since no one understood it when he used it, it was resented. But Mrs Mayton never allowed more than three minutes to go by without a word; and so when the new silence had reached its allotted span, she turned to
30   Penbury and asked:

'Was that Mr Wainwright who went out a little time ago?'

Penbury looked at her oddly.

'What makes you ask that?' he said.

'Well, I was just wondering.'

'I see,' answered Penbury slowly. The atmosphere seemed to tighten,
5 but Miss Wicks went on knitting. 'And are you all wondering?'

'We decided perhaps he'd gone out to post a letter,' murmured Bella.

'No, Wainwright hasn't gone out to post a letter,' responded Penbury.
'He's dead.'

The effect was instantaneous and galvanic. Bella gave a tiny shriek. Mrs
10 Mayton's eyes became two startled glass marbles. Monty Smith opened
his mouth and kept it open. Mr Calthrop, in a split second, lost all
inclination to doze. Miss Wicks looked definitely interested, though she
did not stop knitting. That meant nothing, however. She had promised to
knit at her funeral.
15 'Dead?' gasped Mr Calthrop.

'Dead,' repeated Penbury. 'He is lying on the floor of his room. He is
rather a nasty mess.'

Monty leapt up, and then sat down again.

'You – don't mean . . . ?' he gulped.
20 'That is exactly what I mean,' replied Penbury.

There had been countless silences in Mrs Mayton's drawing-room, but
never a silence like this one. Miss Wicks broke it.

'Shouldn't the police be sent for?' she suggested.

'The police have already been sent for,' said Penbury. 'I phoned the
25 station just before coming into the room.'

'God bless my soul!' said Mr Calthrop.

'How long – that is – when do you expect . . . ?' stammered Monty.

'The police? I should say in two or three minutes,' responded Penbury.
His voice suddenly shed its cynicism and became practical. 'Shall we try
30 and make use of these two or three minutes? We shall all be questioned,
and perhaps we can clear up a little ground before they arrive.'

Mr Calthrop bridled.

'But this is nothing to do with any of us, sir!' he exclaimed.

'The police will not necessarily accept our word for it,' answered
35 Penbury. 'That is why I propose that we consider our alibis in advance. I
am not a doctor, but I estimate from my brief examination of the body
that it has not been dead more than an hour. It could not, of course, be
more than an hour and a half,' he went on, glancing at the clock, 'since it is
now ten past nine, and at twenty to eight we saw him leave the

2

dining-room for his bedroom . . .'

'How do you know he went to his bedroom?' interrupted Miss Wicks.

'Because, having a headache, I followed him upstairs to go to mine for some aspirin, and my room is immediately opposite his,' Penbury

5 explained. 'Now, if my assumption is correct, he was killed between ten minutes past eight and ten minutes past nine, so anyone who can prove that he or she has remained in this room during all that time should have no worry.'

He looked around inquiringly.

10 'We've all been out of the room,' Miss Wicks announced for the company.

'That is unfortunate,' murmured Penbury.

'But so have *you!*' exclaimed Monty, with nervous aggression.

'Yes – so I have,' replied Penbury. 'Then let me give my alibi first. At

15 twenty minutes to eight I followed Wainwright up to the second floor. Before going into his room he made an odd remark which – in the circumstances – is worth repeating. "There's somebody in this house who doesn't like me very much," he said. "Only one?" I answered. "You're luckier than I am." Then he went into his room, and that was the last time

20 I saw him alive. I went into my room. I took two aspirin tablets. I went into the bathroom to wash them down with a drink of water. By the way, my water-bottle again needs filling, Mrs Mayton. Then as my head was still bad, I thought a stroll would be a good idea, and I went out. I kept out till – approximately – nine o'clock. Then I came back. The door you heard

25 closing, Mrs Mayton, was not Wainwright going out. It was me coming in.'

'Wait a moment!' ejaculated Bella.

'Yes?'

'How did you know Mrs Mayton heard the front door close? You weren't here!'

30 Penbury regarded her with interest and respect.

'Intelligent,' he murmured.

'Now, then, don't take too long thinking of an answer!' glared Mr Calthrop.

'I don't need any time at all to think of an answer,' retorted Penbury. 'I

35 know because I listened outside the door. But may I finish my statement in my own way? Thank you! As I say, I came back. I went up to my room.' He paused. 'On the floor I found a handkerchief. It wasn't mine. It hadn't been there when I left. I wondered whether it was Wainwright's – whether he'd been poking around. I went into his room to ask if the handkerchief

3

was his. I found him lying on the ground near his bed. Dressed, of course. On his back. Head towards the window, one arm stretched towards the fireplace. Stabbed through the heart. But no sign of what he'd been stabbed with . . . It looks to me a small wound, but deep. It found the spot
5   all right . . . The window was closed and fastened. Whoever did it entered through the door. I left the room and locked the door. I knew no one should go in again till the police and police doctor turned up. I decided to make sure that no one did. I came down. The telephone, as you know, is in the dining-room. Most inconvenient. It should be in the hall. Passing the
10   drawing-room door I listened, to hear what you all were talking about. I heard Mrs Mayton say, "I wonder where Mr Wainwright's gone?" You, Smith, answered, "Did he go?" And Mrs Mayton replied, "I thought I heard the front door close." Then I went into the dining-room and telephoned the police. And then I joined you.'
15   Flushed and emotional, Mrs Mayton challenged him.

'Why did you sit here for three minutes without telling us?' she demanded.

'I was watching you,' answered Penbury, coolly.

'Well, I call that a rotten alibi!' exclaimed Mr Calthrop. 'Who's to
20   prove you were out all that time?'

'At half past eight I had a cup of coffee at the coffee-stall in Junkers Street,' replied Penbury. 'That's over a mile away. It's not proof, I admit, but they know me there, you see, and it may help. Well, who's next?'

'I am', said Bella. 'I left the room to blow my nose. I went to my room
25   for a handkerchief. And here it *is!*' she concluded, producing it triumphantly.

'How long were you out of the room?' pressed Penbury.

'Five minutes, I should say,' she answered.

'A long time to get a handkerchief?'
30   'Perhaps. But I not only blew my nose, I powdered it.'

'That sounds good enough,' admitted Penbury. 'Would you oblige next, Mr Calthrop? We all know you walk in your sleep. A week ago you walked into my room, didn't you? Have *you* lost a handkerchief?'

Mr Calthrop glared.
35   'What the devil are you implying?' he exclaimed.

'Has Mr Calthrop dozed during the past hour?' pressed Penbury.

'Suppose I have?' he cried. 'What – what damned rubbish! Did I leave this room without knowing it, and kill Wainwright for – for no reason at all during forty winks?' He swallowed, and calmed down. 'I left the room, sir, about twenty minutes ago to fetch the evening paper from the dining-room to do the crossword puzzle!' He tapped it viciously. 'Here it is!'

Penbury shrugged his shoulders.

5   'I should be the last person to refute such an emphatic statement,' he said, 'but let me suggest that you give the statement to the police with slightly less emphasis, Mr Smith?'

Monty Smith had followed the conversation anxiously, and he had his story ready. He had rehearsed it three times in his mind, and he was not 10 going to make Mr Calthrop's mistake. Speaking slowly and carefully – he knew that if he spoke fast he would stutter – he answered:

'This is why I left the room. I suddenly remembered that I'd forgotten to return Mr Wainwright's latchkey. He'd lent it to me this afternoon, when I lost mine. But when I got as far as the first floor I met Mrs Mayton, 15 who asked me to help her with the curtain of the landing window. It had come off some of its hooks. I did so and then returned to the drawing-room with her. You'll remember, all of you, that we returned together.'

'That's right,' nodded Mrs Mayton. 'And the reason *I* went out was to 20 fix the curtain.'

Penbury looked at Monty hard.

'What about that latchkey?' he demanded.

'Eh? Oh, of course,' jerked Monty. 'The curtain put it out of my mind. I came down with it still in my pocket.'

25 'Then you've got it now?'

'Yes.'

'And you didn't go up to his room?'

'No! Thank goodness! I've just said so, haven't I?'

Penbury shrugged his shoulders again. He did not seem satisfied. But 30 he turned now to Miss Wicks, and the old lady inquired, while her needles moved busily.

'My turn?'

'If you'll be so good,' answered Penbury. 'Just as a matter of form.'

'Yes, I quite understand,' she replied, smiling. 'There's no need to 35 apologize. Well, I left the drawing-room to fetch some knitting-needles. The steel ones I'm using now. My room, as of course you know, is also on the second floor, the little side-room, and after I'd got the needles I was just about to come down when I heard Mr Wainwright's cough . . .'

'What! You heard him cough?' interrupted Penbury. 'What

time was that?'

'Just before nine, I think it was,' said Miss Wicks. 'Oh, that irritating cough! How it gets on one's nerves, doesn't it? Or I should say, how it *did* get on one's nerves. Morning, noon and night. And he wouldn't do anything for it. Enough to send one mad.'

She paused. The tense atmosphere grew suddenly tenser.

'Go on,' murmured Penbury.

'I'm going on,' answered Miss Wicks. 'Why not? Your door was open, Mr Penbury, and I went in to ask if we couldn't do something about it. But you were out. You've just told us where. And suddenly, when I heard Mr Wainwright coughing again across the passage – that awful clicking sound it always ended with – well, I felt I couldn't stand it any more, and I was knocking at his door almost before I knew it. It was my handkerchief you found in your room, Mr Penbury. I must have dropped it there.'

She paused again. Again Penbury murmured, 'Go on.'

She turned on him with sudden ferocity. Mr Calthrop nearly jumped out of his chair. Monty felt perspiration dripping down his neck. Bella twined her fingers together to prevent herself from shrieking. Mrs Mayton sat rigid.

'Will you stop interrupting?' shouted the old woman.

Penbury moistened his lips. For a few moments Miss Wicks knitted rapidly, the steel points of the needles making the only sound in the room. They seemed to be doing a venomous dance. Then she continued, in a queer hard voice.

' "Come in," called Mr Wainwright. "I'm coming in," I called back. And I went in. And there he stood smiling at me. "You haven't come to complain of my cough again, have you?" he asked. "No," I answered. "I've come to cure it." And I plunged a steel knitting-needle into his heart – like this!'

She stretched out a bony hand, and, with amazing strength, stabbed a cushion.

The next instant there came a knocking on the front door. 'The police!' gasped Mr Calthrop. But no one moved. With tense ears they listened to the maid ascending from the basement, they heard the front door open, they heard footsteps entering . . .

A moment later they heard Mr Wainwright's cough.

'Yes, and I heard it when he went out ten minutes ago,' smiled Miss Wicks. 'But thank you very much indeed, Mr Penbury. I was as bored as the rest of them.'

6

Questions

The Author

J. Jefferson Farjeon (1883–1956) was born in London, one of a family of four, all of whom were writers. He is best known for his mystery stories and was one of the first modern authors to mix romance and humour with crime.

The Story

Waiting for the Police is set in a boarding-house where nothing ever happens to make life more exciting for the odd collection of people who live there. But one of the guests manages to think of something which does stir up quite a bit of interest. Where is Mr Wainwright? The plot is well laid, the language is very descriptive and the style is neat, with short sentences and a well-balanced dialogue.

Points to Consider

While reading the story, think about the following:

(a) Mr Penbury's control of the situation in the drawing-room.
(b) how the other characters react to what is happening – when they show interest, when they feel shocked, when they show fear, and so on.
(c) the author's humour.

Listening Comprehension

Choose the correct answer or complete the sentences in the following (1,1–2,31):

1 Who was the first person to enquire about Mr Wainwright?

a Miss Wicks.
b Mrs Mayton.
c Mr Penbury.
d Bella.

2 For board and lodging, Mr Wainwright paid

    a three pounds a week.
    b one pound a day.
    c three guineas a week.
    d one pound a week.

3 How long had Miss Wicks been knitting for?

    a 17 years.
    b 7 years.
    c 70 years.
    d 27 years.

4 What was Mr Calthrop doing when the conversation about Mr Wainwright began?

    a Looking out of the window.
    b Reading the evening paper.
    c Having a sleep.
    d Thinking about the problems of middle-age.

5 Mrs Mayton was a woman who was known for

    a speaking very little.
    b nearly always talking.
    c not saying anything.
    d keeping everybody talking.

6 What was Miss Wicks' usual occupation?

    a Doing crosswords.
    b Sewing.
    c Knitting.
    d Reading novels.

7 Who suggested sending for the police?

    a Bella.
    b Monty Smith.
    c Mrs Mayton.
    d Miss Wicks.

Reading Comprehension

I

Complete the following sentences in your own words (1,1–2,31):

1 Monty Smith always tried very hard to . . .
2 Miss Wicks thought that perhaps Mr Wainwright had gone out to . . .
3 Mrs Mayton thought it was Mr Penbury who had gone out, because . . .
4 When Mr Penbury walked into the drawing-room, the conversation . . .
5 All the time that Mr Penbury was talking, Miss Wicks . . .
6 The news about Mr Wainwright made Monty Smith . . .
7 Miss Wicks suggested that . . .
8 Mr Penbury said that the police would be arriving . . .

II

After reading the whole story, answer these questions:

1 How long did Mr Penbury think the body had been dead?
2 At what time was Mr Wainwright seen leaving the dining-room?
3 Why did Penbury go up to his bedroom?
4 How many tablets did Penbury take?
5 Why did Penbury go for a walk after taking the tablets?
6 When Penbury went up to his room again, what did he find on the floor?
7 Where in the house was the telephone?
8 Why did Mr Calthrop leave the room?
9 What did Monty Smith say he suddenly remembered?
10 What was wrong with the landing curtain?
11 Why did Miss Wicks leave the drawing-room?
12 Whose handkerchief was it that Penbury found on the floor?

III

Fill in the appropriate preposition from the list below:

between, for, in, at, with, by, through, beside, near, of, on, about, without, to

1 Mrs Mayton had a conversation . . . Mr Penbury.
2 All that mattered . . . Miss Wicks was her knitting.
3 The handkerchief was lying . . . the floor.
4 It seemed that Bella was very angry . . . Mrs Mayton.
5 I found him lying . . . the ground . . . his bed.
6 I went . . . to ask if we couldn't do something . . . it.

Discussion

1 Which of all the characters did you like best? Give your reasons.
2 Describe in two or three sentences two of the other characters in the story.
3 Discuss the kind of relationship which existed between the guests at the boarding-house. Comment on their loyalty to one another and their mistrust of one another, for example.
4 Were you surprised by the ending? Did you think the ending should have been different?

Written work

Write a short letter giving a brief account of a recent stay at a boarding-house or at a hotel.

OR

Choose a character in the story and make a note of all the phrases which describe him or her. Then write a short paragraph of not more than 150 words describing the character you have chosen.

Role-play

Polite conversation
Divide up into pairs or into groups of three. Pretend you are sitting in the drawing-room of a hotel on a rainy summer's evening talking to each other about general topics such as the weather, holidays, the family, and so on. See how long you can keep up the conversation.

Grammar Points

I there is/it is

'There is somebody in this house who doesn't like me very much.' (3,17)
'On the floor I found a handkerchief. It wasn't mine. It hadn't been there when I left.' (3,37)

There refers to a noun or pronoun later in the sentence.
It refers to a noun or pronoun in the previous sentence.

10

Complete the following sentences with *it* or *there*:

1 ... was a young lady called Bella staying in Mrs Mayton's boarding-house.
2 Life in the boarding-house was not very interesting. In fact, ... was very dull.
3 ... was nothing anyone could do to stop the police coming.
4 Mr Penbury went up to his room. ... was opposite Mr Wainwright's.
5 ... was a handkerchief on the floor of Mr Penbury's room.
6 ... was a knock on the front door. ... wasn't the police as they all thought.

II for/during

She had knitted *for* seventy years. (1,12)
Has Mr Calthrop dozed *during* the past hour?

For answers the question 'How long?'.
During answers the question 'When?'.

Mini-dialogue
A: When did you go to Paris?
B: During the summer.
A: How long were you there for?
B: I was there for about six weeks.

Divide up into pairs. Choose suitable words from the lists below and act out the dialogue:

A: London	**B:** his illness	**B:** two hours
town	the Christmas holidays	a whole day
the country	this week	ten days
his house	the summer	the weekend

III Verbs of sensation + object + -ing

Monty felt perspiration dripping down his neck. (6,17)
... they listened to the maid ascending from the basement. (6,34)

Rewrite the following sentences using a similar construction:

1 John heard Peter. He was shouting for help.
2 Mary saw Michael at the next table. He was eating a sandwich.
3 The dog barked at the door. Everyone could hear it.
4 The children tried to get into the greenhouse. We watched them from an upstairs window.
5 The rain was coming through Julia's coat. She could feel it.

11

6 Ann heard the phone. It rang while she was in the garden.
7 The cake was burning in the oven. I could smell it.

Words and Phrases

I

her second-floor back: the man living in the back room on the second
floor of her boarding-house. (1,3)
board and lodging: a room and meals. (1,4)
whip up a little interest: try to arouse interest. (1,6)
keep any ball rolling: keep any conversation going once it had been
started. (1,9)
the boarding-house lovely: the beauty of the boarding-house. (1,15)
middle-aged doze: light sleep in a chair often taken by middle-aged
people. (1,19)
He possessed a brain: he was clever. (1,26)
the station: here, office of the local police force. (2,25)
clear up a little ground: get the facts clear. (2,31)
bridled: showed that he was offended by throwing up his head and
drawing in his chin. (2,32)
he'd been poking around: he'd been looking around where he shouldn't
have been. (3,39)
challenged: demanded an explanation. (4,15)
Would you oblige next?: Would you be kind enough to help us next?
(4,31)
viciously: in a bad temper. (5,2)
jerked: said suddenly. (5,23)
a matter of form: something which has to be done, but which is not really
necessary. (5,33)
doing a venomous dance: moving up and down in a very
dangerous-looking way. (6,23)

II

Make a list of all the words in the story describing the way people spoke,
e.g. *gasped* (2,15), *gulped* (2,19). Then try to categorize them under
certain headings – shock, agreement, etc.

Dickon and David

Laurence Lerner

Tamsin pressed her left thumb against the metal catch, and let it squeeze the flesh inwards. Nothing happened, so she tried to press harder. The obstinacy of objects lay, as always, in front of her: she never knew whether her actions would overcome it, or slip past it, or subside exhausted. Just as her fingers were giving up she heard a click, and the bag flew open. She sighed, and moved her attention from the tired fingers to the whole shape and surface of her body. Carefully, she paid attention to the sunlight, crinkling over her skin. It was warm: the wind came off the sea, salty and fresh, but did not make her shiver. Things were not really too much trouble, in the end. She had not had to struggle long, and the bag lay open on her lap. In a few moments, she would feel strong enough to rummage inside. A warm feeling of deserved achievement washed over her.

The old man next to her was talking. He must have been talking for quite a while, because none of his sentences sounded like beginnings. It didn't matter: he would be talking about himself. If anything mattered, he would say it again. But it couldn't matter to her. This wasn't the bench she usually sat on.

'I don't usually sit on this bench,' he was saying. 'I walk down to the next lot. Just the right distance. I sit on the side facing the sea – if it's warm enough. But today's rather chilly.' He looked at her. 'Isn't it?' he added, plaintively.

'It's perfectly warm,' said Tamsin. 'It's the warmest day we've had so far.'

'I feel chilly,' he said. 'I didn't feel strong enough to walk to the next bench. But this one's not so comfortable.' He turned laboriously to face her. 'There's a hole in one of the slats,' he said accusingly. 'I can feel the splinters.'

'I don't usually sit here,' said Tamsin, 'I sit in my garden. I've got a perfectly good garden.' She looked out at the barren, puckered sea, flowering in little waves. 'Forsythia,' she said. 'Anemones. And two rose bushes.'

'I don't know why it is,' he said. 'I just didn't feel up to walking to the next bench.'

She listened to the traces of his voice before speaking. 'It's perfectly simple,' she said. 'You're too old.'

5 'Well I'm old. Of course I'm old. I'm older than you, I'm sure. But I'm not *too* old.'

'You're not older than me,' she asserted.

'Eighty-one,' he said. 'Eighty-one next month. My wife died ten years ago. I look after myself.'

10 'I'll bet you don't. I'll bet your room's full of washing-up, right at this moment. Dirty dishes everywhere. On the table, or the window-sill. Everywhere.'

'It's not easy, doing it all. People don't realize. Not when you're over eighty. And I walk down to the sea every day. To the next bench, usually.'

15 'I'm eighty-six,' she said contemptuously. 'I've got six grandchildren. One of them's a student. She digs the garden.' She began looking through her handbag. She was feeling stronger now, she could run her fingers through the rustle and tumble of contents without feeling nausea.

'Students,' spluttered the man. 'I've got no time for students. Always 20 up to something.'

She had hold of an envelope and was lifting it out of the bag. But it wasn't the right one. She could feel the furry surface of paper that had been in her bag a long time.

'My neighbour's got a son,' the man was saying. 'You can tell he's a 25 student. Great baggy trousers, like skirts. And hair.' His breath started to come quicker and noisier. 'How do you tell boys from girls nowadays?' The wheezing quickened, it joined the family of laughs. 'That one's a boy all right.'

Reluctantly she let go of the velvety envelope. She would have liked to 30 take it out and stroke it a few times. But she would do that later; first she had to find the other one.

'I'll bet you don't know what my name is,' he said.

Her fingers had found the stiffer corner of another envelope. It was cooler, smoother. That would be it.

35 'You know what my name is?' he asked again. He seemed quite prepared to say everything several times. 'My Christian name?'

She let the envelope go. She could take it out soon enough, when she felt ready to read it again. She was in no hurry. The breeze touched her right cheek as she turned to look at the old man: a salty flick on the skin.

14

'John,' she said. 'Or Peter. Something like that.'

He chuckled in delight. 'That's what you think.'

'They probably call you Jack. Or Pete.' She couldn't make out the features very well, she only had the voice to go on. 'Or Fred. Or even Alf, I wouldn't be surprised.'

'Dickon,' he said. 'My name's Dickon. I bet you've never even heard that, have you?' He waited a moment, then said, more angrily, 'Have you?'

'Have I what?' she said, suddenly tired.

'Dickon,' he said. 'Did you even know that was a name?'

There were a dozen or so white triangles moving over the roughened sea, two of them with red stripes. Why wasn't she in her canvas chair, on the back lawn? Yesterday she'd been sitting watching the forsythia. She could still feel in her back the moment she'd bent to pick up two or three yellow blossoms from the lawn. Her fingers had not wanted to grip firmly, one had swum idly back down on to the grass. Like that yacht, she thought, like that striped sail swimming idly over the rough water. She must have walked down here, earlier this morning. By herself?

'It's a very old name. My wife used to say, "What on earth came over your Dad, to give you such a funny name?" She used to think he'd made it up.'

All she wanted was to watch the forsythia swaying over her head. Blurring. But she couldn't now.

'It's short for Richard. It's an old form of Dick. But Jane used to think it was made up. She was very ignorant, in some ways, was Jane. You know, even King Richard III was called Dickon. There's even a rhyme about him, I'll recite it to you if you're interested.'

She took the letter out of her bag. Yes, this was the one, you could feel it had only come today, and had only been read once. She drew out the stiff paper, hearing it hiss as it rubbed against the envelope. Nice bit of paper Mary had used, no cheap rubbish. It creaked as she opened it out.

'It goes like this. Just listen now.' His voice grew tauter, rose in pitch, as he prepared to recite. '*Dickon of England don't be so bold, For Dickon of England is bought and sold.*' He waved his hands, conducting. 'That was a famous old rhyme once. It comes in Shakespeare.'

He paused for effect; and the white triangles dodged and swung in the sunshine. Tamsin held the letter on her lap, gathering courage.

'My Dad was very interested in names. He used to say we ought to keep the good old names alive. We ought to know where they came from, we ought to go on using them. You know what he called my sister. Dorcas. I suppose you've never heard that one either. It's in the Bible.'

'You seem very sure about what I haven't heard of.'

5 'He didn't have any time for all these modern names, like Christine or Gladys. All this rubbish they get from the TV.' He turned to her and wheezed. 'I hope your name's not Gladys.'

'No,' she said, staring out to sea. 'No, it's not.'

'My daughter's called Gloria,' he said in disgust. 'Couldn't stop my
10 wife. She wouldn't hear of any of the good old names. Tabitha, I wanted to call her. Or Edith. Or at any rate Mary. But she was very obstinate, was Jane. She kept insisting Dickon was a made-up name. You couldn't argue with her.'

The letter was open on her lap but of course she couldn't read it. The
15 words were lumpish and irregular on the page, and as she screwed up her eyes (she could never stop herself – as if that would help) they blurred and slid about. There was no way of coaxing them into shapes she could read. She would have to find her glasses.

'Takes after her mother, does Gloria. Got it in for men. You should see
20 the dance she leads her husband. If he so much as reads the paper.'

'I live with my granddaughter,' said Tamsin defensively. 'She's been good to me.'

'Gloria, she's called. Goes to show, doesn't it?'

'She looks after the garden, she brings me my breakfast in bed. She's a
25 good girl, is Mary. Not like the others.'

'I wonder if I could get as far as the other bench. It's much more comfortable.' The old man had suddenly lost interest in the conversation; he shifted restlessly on the hard slats.

'Of course she's on to a good thing.' Suddenly afraid he would go away,
30 Tamsin began to talk very fast. 'I mean, the house is mine, she doesn't pay any rent. She has everything free, hot water, bedding, everything. On the telephone all day to young men, I pay it all. And she knows I'll leave it to her.'

She could hear a slight choking from the old man. He was pushing with
35 his hands against the slats, trying to get himself up. Then with a gasp he relaxed, and sat down again on the bench, looking out at the sails and the dazzle. 'I ought to try,' he said hopelessly.

She had found her spectacles. She drew them out of her bag, and quickly pushed the bag shut. It was only last week she had spilt the whole

16

contents of the bag on to the grass, when Mary was out. It had taken hours to find everything, and then Mary had had to help her up off the ground when she came back. But there had been no need to go on as if she'd spilt it on purpose.

The bag safely shut she had to open the spectacle case. Her right thumb had to run along the edge, then when it lifted enough she pushed her left thumb under the lid. She could feel the sting where she'd cut herself last week, trying to chop the onions. It had been to save Mary trouble, but she hadn't been at all grateful. Had told her to leave the cooking alone. Where would Mary be now, if she'd always left the cooking alone?

By now the glasses were on her nose, and she shook out the letter till it lay flat on her lap. She enjoyed the stiffness of the page, and its rigid folds; always used the best, her family. Something stirred uneasily in her head as she thought that, as if it wasn't true any more. She had a vague feeling that the letter didn't belong with the wide view, the warmth, the slight tingle of the breeze. As if it was an indoor letter, and ought to be read in bed. With the fire on, even.

Then when the words stood still, and she saw the shapes that she knew said, Dear Grannie, then she remembered. It didn't matter that even with glasses the shapes were blurred, and had to be held down till they fitted a word. There was no need to read it, she knew what it said, even if she couldn't remember the exact words. And in fact, she could even remember the words. Each one, as she made it out that morning, had clung, had clipped itself to her memory. 'Dear Grannie,' Mary had written, 'There's no point in beating about the bush. You know I'm on holiday with David, and he's asked me to marry him. Of course I've said "Yes", I know you didn't like David but you must realize that you were prejudiced. I'm going to move in with him as soon as we get back, and we'll get married in June. So I shan't be living with you any more, Grannie. I'm sorry about this, but you must understand it was getting difficult anyway. And I don't know that you're really able to stay in the house by yourself any more. This is a real problem, and we'll have to talk about it very seriously when I get back. I'm having a wonderful time. Much love, Mary.'

The old man had managed to stand up, swaying slightly. 'Well,' he said, 'I'll be going now. I don't think I'll walk to the next bench after all, it seems far enough to get home.' He turned towards her, blotting out the sails. 'And remember,' he said, 'you can tell people you've met someone called Dickon.'

She looked up at him, suddenly hearing very distinctly everything he was saying. 'Listen,' she said, 'do you know what *my* name is?' She had seized hold of his arms, and was pulling herself up. 'It's Tamsin.' She was surprised at how easily she got up, till she realized that she was pulling him down. 'It's a Cornish form, the name is Thomasin. It's quite as old as Dickon.' He collapsed heavily on to the bench beside her, just managing to turn enough to sit down and not fall face forwards. 'But it's no use keeping the old names, you can't stop fashion. Now they all call their daughters June. I ask you. Or Lorna.'

'Or Gloria,' he panted.

'Or Gloria. Or they call boys David. I ask you. Sounds old because it comes in the Bible, but it isn't. No one ever called their boys David till nowadays. It's a fake name, that's what it is, a fraud.' She turned it over in her mouth, and spat it out at the sea. 'David. David.'

Questions

The Author

Laurence Lerner was born in 1925 and has been Professor of English at Sussex University. He is well known as a poet and a short story writer. His works include A.R.T.H.U.R: *The Life and Opinions of a Digital Computer* (1974). *Dickon and David* first appeared in the review Encounter in February 1977.

The Story

Dickon and David is about two old people who meet each other for the first time on a seaside bench. While reading the story notice the difference in their attitudes to life, their difference in temperament and their different life-styles. Notice also how the feelings of the characters come across through the dialogue in the story.

Points to Consider

While reading the story, think about the following:

(*a*) the way in which the two old people each seem to live in a world of their own.
(*b*) the author's way of describing the old people's behaviour, their feelings towards each other, etc.
(*c*) the different prejudices of Tamsin and Dickon.

Listening Comprehension

True or false? (13,1–14,28)

1 The old man had only just started talking when Tamsin opened her bag.
2 Tamsin did not usually sit on this bench.
3 The old man thought that this bench was less comfortable than his usual one.
4 Tamsin was younger than the old man.
5 The old man liked students a lot.

Reading Comprehension

I

Complete the sentences in the following:

1 The sentence 'he turned laboriously to face her' (13,26) means that Dickon was

   a very tired.
   b feeling pleased with himself.
   c unable to hear very well.
   d unable to move easily.

2 The word barren in 'the barren, puckered sea' (13,30) suggests that the sea was

   a very rough.
   b full of ships.
   c completely deserted.
   d like a garden.

3 Dickon didn't feel like walking to the next bench because

   a it was too cold.
   b he wanted to go home.
   c he hadn't enough time.
   d he wasn't feeling up to it.

4 When Tamsin said contemptuously 'I'm eighty-six' (14,15), it shows that she

   a was tired of being old.
   b did not have much respect for Dickon's age.
   c was thinking of her childhood.
   d was proud of her age.

II

Complete the following sentences in your own words (13,1–14,28):

1 When Tamsin did not sit on the bench by the sea, she . . .
2 Tamsin thought the old man's room would be . . .
3 Tamsin began looking through her handbag to . . .
4 The old man could tell his neighbour's son was a student because . . .
5 After finding the envelope she was looking for, Tamsin . . .

20

III

After reading the whole story, answer these questions:

1 Where had Tamsin been sitting watching the forsythia?
2 Who gave the old man his name? His mother or his father?
3 Who wrote the rhyme that Dickon recites about his name?
4 Who is Gloria?
5 Is Tamsin's granddaughter kind to her?
6 How much does Mary pay for accommodation?
7 What had Tamsin spilt on the grass the previous week?
8 What did Mary say she was going to do in June?
9 Had Tamsin ever met David?
10 What is Tamsin short for? Where does the name come from?

Discussion

1 Did you feel sad or happy when you finished reading the story? Why? What did you think of the two characters? Did you like one better than the other? Why?
2 How can you tell from their behaviour that Tamsin and Dickon are old?
3 What does the old man think about students? Do you agree?
4 For a long time the two people seem to be talking at each other, not to each other. What is Dickon interested in? What about Tamsin?
5 Describe Tamsin's relationship with Mary. In what way does the letter change things?
6 At the end of the story, Tamsin suddenly hears what the old man is saying, and the two old people can agree about their dislike of certain names. What does the name Gloria signify to Dickon? What does the name David signify to Tamsin?

Role-play

Choose two students to prepare and then act the dialogue in the story from 'I'll bet you don't know what my name is' (14,32) to 'Did you even know that was a name?' (15,10) Do not read out the narrative.

OR

Talk to the student next to you about your respective names and what you know about them. Would you prefer to be called by another name?

General Discussion

This is a story about old people, their feelings of loneliness and of being let down by the younger generation – of not being wanted any more. How do you feel about this problem? What do you think might be the solution? Should old people live alone? With their children? Or in special homes for old people?

Grammar Points

I Adjectives and adverbs

'But today's rather chilly.'
'Isn't it?' he added, plaintively.
'It's perfectly warm,' said Tamsin. (13,23)

Alter the form of the adjectives and adverbs in brackets in the following passage where necessary:

Tamsin was quite (*comfortable*) on the wooden bench. The wind was (*warm*) and the sun shone (*bright*). Dickon was not sitting (*comfortable*). He could (*easy*) feel the splinters in one of the slats. He (*usual*) sat on another bench farther along, but he didn't feel (*terrible*) (*strong*) today, so he rather (*unwilling*) stayed where he was. Tamsin was rummaging (*laborious*) in her bag, looking for her granddaughter's letter. She had been (*extreme*) (*sad*) to get it, after all she had done for Mary. Children were never (*grateful*), she thought (*sad*). It was so (*hard*) to be old, even if she tried very (*hard*) not to act old.

II Possessive pronouns with parts of the body and clothing

Tamsin pressed her left thumb against the metal catch. (13,1)
The bag lay open on her lap. (13,11)

Put in the correct possessive pronoun in the following sentences:

1 He looked at . . . nails.
2 Tamsin felt the wind in . . . hair.
3 Tamsin felt something stirring uneasily in . . . head.
4 Dickon waved . . . hands about.
5 The old people put . . . hands in . . . pockets.
6 If we go out now, . . . feet will get wet.

Words and Phrases

I

the obstinacy of objects: the refusal of things to give way to her, to do as she wanted them to. (13,3)

crinkling over her skin: showing up the wrinkles. (13,8)

a feeling . . . washed over her: a feeling spread through her. (13,12)

feel up to walking: feel strong enough to walk. (14,1)

the rustle and tumble of contents: the different sounds and feel of things being moved about in her bag. (14,18)

joined the family of laughs: turned into laughter. (14,27)

only the voice to go on: only the voice to use as a guide. (15,4)

one (blossom) had swum idly: had floated slowly. (15,16)

What on earth came over your Dad?; What made your Dad do that? (15,19)

Blurring: becoming unclear and diffuse. (15,23)

King Richard III: King of England, 1452–1485. (15,26)

His voice . . . rose in pitch: his voice became higher, more like a woman's. (15,33)

for effect: to make an impression on Tamsin. (15,37)

the white triangles dodged: the white sails of the boats moved about backwards and forwards. (15,37)

The words were lumpish: the letters of the words seemed to go together in lumps. (16,15)

Got it in for men: she dislikes men and shows it. (16,19)

You should see the dance she leads her husband: you should see how difficult she makes life for her husband. (16,19)

Goes to show, doesn't it?: it just shows you she is not as nice as her name sounds. (16,23)

she's on to a good thing: she has a lot to gain. (16,29)

leave it to her: leave everything to her when I die. (16,32)

the dazzle: the very bright light, sunshine. (16,37)

there had been no need to go on: she need not have kept up such an angry attitude. (17,3)

blotting out the sails: hiding the sails from view. (17,37)

II

Make a list of all the adverbs and phrases used in the story, describing the way either Tamsin or Dickon feel about things or say things, e.g. *he added plaintively* (13,21), *he turned laboriously* (13,26). Try to categorize them under headings such as anger, sorrow, and so on.

The Last Tea

Dorothy Parker

The young man in the chocolate-brown suit sat down at the table, where
the girl with the artificial camellia had been sitting for forty minutes.
   'Guess I must be late,' he said. 'Sorry you been waiting.'
   'Oh, goodness!' she said. 'I just got here myself, just about a second
5   ago. I simply went ahead and ordered because I was dying for a cup of tea.
I was late, myself. I haven't been here more than a minute.'
   'That's good,' he said. 'Hey, hey, easy on the sugar – one lump is fair
enough. And take away those cakes. Terrible! Do I feel terrible!'
   'Ah,' she said, 'you do? Ah. Whadda matter?'
10   'Oh, I'm ruined,' he said. 'I'm in terrible shape.'
   'Ah, the poor boy,' she said, 'Was it feelin' mizzable? Ah, and it came
way up here to meet me! You shouldn't have done that – I'd have
understood. Ah, just think of it coming all the way up here when it's so
sick!'
15   'Oh, that's all right,' he said. 'I might as well be here as any place
else. Any place is like any other place, the way I feel today. Oh, I'm all
shot.'
   'Why, that's just awful,' she said. 'Why, you poor sick thing. Goodness,
I hope it isn't influenza. They say there's a lot of it around.'
20   'Influenza!' he said. 'I wish that was all I had. Oh, I'm poisoned. I'm
through. I'm off the stuff for life. Know what time I got to bed? Twenty
minutes past five, A.M., this morning. What a night! What an evening!'
   'I thought,' she said, 'that you were going to stay at the office and work
late. You said you'd be working every night this week.'
25   'Yeah, I know,' he said. 'But it gave me the jumps, thinking about going
down there and sitting at that desk. I went up to May's – she was throwing
a party. Say, there was somebody there said they knew you.'
   'Honestly?' she said. 'Man or woman?'
   'Dame,' he said. 'Name's Carol McCall. Say, why haven't I been told
30   about her before? That's what I call a girl. What a looker she is!'
   'Oh, really?' she said. 'That's funny – I never heard of anyone that

thought that. I've heard people say she was sort of nice-looking, if she
wouldn't make up so much. But I never heard of anyone that thought she
was pretty.'

'Pretty is right,' he said. 'What a couple of eyes she's got on her!'

5   'Really?' she said. 'I never noticed them particularly. But I haven't seen
her for a long time – sometimes people change, or something.'

'She says she used to go to school with you,' he said.

'Well, we went to the same school,' she said. 'I simply happened to go to
public school because it happened to be right near us, and Mother hated

10   to have me crossing streets. But she was three or four classes ahead of me.
She's ages older than I am.'

'She's three or four classes ahead of them all,' he said. 'Dance! Can she
step! "Burn your clothes, baby," I kept telling her. I must have been fried
pretty.'

15   'I was out dancing myself, last night,' she said. 'Wally Dillon and I. He's
just been pestering me to go out with him. He's the most wonderful
dancer. Goodness! I didn't get home until I don't know what time. I must
look just simply a wreck. Don't I?'

'You look all right,' he said.

20   'Wally's crazy,' she said. 'The things he says! For some crazy reason or
other, he's got it into his head that I've got beautiful eyes, and, well, he
just kept talking about them till I didn't know where to look, I was so
embarrassed. I got so red, I thought everybody in the place would be
looking at me. I got just as red as a brick. Beautiful eyes! Isn't he

25   crazy?'

'He's all right,' he said. 'Say, this little McCall girl, she's had all kinds of
offers to go into moving pictures. "Why don't you go ahead and go?" I
told her. But she says she doesn't feel like it.'

'There was a man up at the lake, two summers ago,' she said. 'He was a

30   director or something with one of the big moving-picture people – oh, he
had all kinds of influence! – and he used to keep insisting and insisting that
I ought to be in the movies. Said I ought to be doing sort of Garbo parts. I
used to just laugh at him. Imagine!'

'She's had about a million offers,' he said. 'I told her to go ahead and go.

35   She keeps getting these offers all the time.'

'Oh, really?' she said. 'Oh, listen, I knew I had something to ask you.
Did you call me up last night, by any chance?'

'Me?' he said. 'No, I didn't call you.'

'While I was out, Mother said this man's voice kept calling up,' she said.

'I thought maybe it might be you, by some chance. I wonder who it could have been. Oh – I guess I know who it was. Yes, that's who it was!'

'No, I didn't call you,' he said. 'I couldn't have seen a telephone, last night. What a head I had on me, this morning! I called Carol up, around
5   ten, and she said she was feeling great. Can that girl hold her liquor!'

'It's a funny thing about me,' she said. 'It just makes me feel sort of sick to see a girl drink. It's just something in me, I guess. I don't mind a man so much, but it makes me feel perfectly terrible to see a girl get intoxicated. It's just the way I am, I suppose.'

10   'Does she carry it!' he said. 'And then feels great the next day. There's a girl! Hey, what are you doing there? I don't want any more tea, thanks. I'm not one of these tea boys. And these tea-rooms give me the jumps. Look at all those old dames, will you? Enough to give you the jumps.'

'Of course, if you'd rather be some place, drinking, with I don't know
15   what kinds of people,' she said, 'I'm sure I don't see how I can help that. Goodness, there are enough people that are glad enough to take me to tea. I don't know how many people keep calling me up and pestering me to take me to tea. Plenty of people!'

'All right, all right, I'm here, aren't I?' he said. 'Keep your hair on.'
20   'I could name them all day,' she said.

'All right,' he said. 'What's there to crab about?'

'Goodness, it isn't any of my business what you do,' she said. 'But I hate to see you wasting your time with people that aren't nearly good enough for you. That's all.'

25   'No need worrying over me,' he said. 'I'll be all right. Listen. You don't have to worry.'

'It's just I don't like to see you wasting your time,' she said, 'staying up all night and then feeling terribly the next day. Ah, I was forgetting he was so sick. Ah, I was mean, wasn't I, scolding him when he was so mizzable.
30   Poor boy. How's he feel now?'

'Oh, I'm all right,' he said. 'I feel fine. You want anything else? How about getting a check? I got to make a telephone call before six.'

'Oh, really?' she said. 'Calling up Carol?'

'She said she might be in around now,' he said.
35   'Seeing her tonight?' she said.

'She's going to let me know when I call up,' he said. 'She's probably got about a million dates. Why?'

'I was just wondering,' she said. 'Goodness, I've got to fly! I'm having dinner with Wally, and he's so crazy, he's probably there now. He's called me up about a hundred times today.'

'Wait till I pay the check,' he said, 'and I'll put you on a bus.'

'Oh, don't bother,' she said. 'It's right at the corner. I've got to fly. I suppose you want to stand and call up your friend from here?'

5   'It's an idea,' he said. 'Sure you'll be all right?'

'Oh, sure,' she said. Busily she gathered her gloves and purse, and left her chair. He rose, not quite fully, as she stopped beside him.

'When'll I see you again?' she said.

'I'll call you up,' he said. 'I'm all tied up, down at the office and
10   everything. Tell you what I'll do. I'll give you a ring.'

'Honestly, I have more dates!' she said. 'It's terrible. I don't know when I'll have a minute. But you call up, will you?'

'I'll do that,' he said. 'Take care of yourself.'

'You take care of yourself,' she said. 'Hope you'll feel all right.'

15   'Oh, I'm fine,' he said. 'Just beginning to come back to life.'

'Be sure and let me know how you feel,' she said. 'Will you? Sure, now? Well, good-by. Oh, have a good time tonight!'

'Thanks,' he said. 'Hope you have a good time, too.'

'Oh, I will,' she said. 'I expect to. I've got to rush! Oh, I nearly forgot!
20   Thanks ever so much for the tea. It was lovely.'

'Be yourself, will you?' he said.

'It was,' she said. 'Well. Now don't forget to call me up, will you? Sure? Well, good-by.'

'Solong,' he said.

25   She walked on down the little lane between the blue-painted tables.

Questions

The Author

Dorothy Parker was born in 1893 and was a poet, satirist and drama critic as well as a short story writer. The *Collected Short Stories*, from which **The Last Tea** is taken, was published in 1939. She died in 1967.

The Story

In **The Last Tea** a young man and a girl meet for a cup of tea in a tea-room. They have been friends for some time, but now something has happened to change things between them.

Points to Consider

While reading the story, think about the following:

(*a*) the behaviour of the young people to each other.
(*b*) the way in which the girl tries to get the young man's interest.
(*c*) the use of slang.

Listening Comprehension

Complete the sentences in the following (24,1–25,11):

1 The girl ordered tea while she waited because

   a she'd waited long enough.
   b she enjoyed tea before a meal.
   c she hated coffee.
   d she was very thirsty.

2 The young man went to bed at

   a 05.25.
   b 20.05.
   c 05.20.
   d 04.40.

3 The young man was attracted to Carol McCall because of

 a her beautiful voice.
 b the way she walked.
 c her good looks.
 d her good education.

4 The girl had gone out with Wally Dillon because

 a they went to the same public school.
 b she wanted to teach him to dance.
 c he had kept on asking her to go out with him.
 d she thought he had beautiful eyes.

Reading Comprehension

I

Choose the correct answer in the following:

1 'I'm in terrible shape' (24,10) means

 a 'My body is too thin'.
 b 'My legs aren't long enough'.
 c 'I don't feel well'.
 d 'I could feel a lot worse'.

2 'But it gave me the jumps' (24,25) refers to

 a the horrible weather they'd had.
 b the long time the girl had waited for a cup of tea.
 c the young man sitting in his office.
 d the young man's feelings about Carol.

3 ' . . . if she wouldn't make up so much,' (25,1) refers to Carol's

 a telling lies.
 b painting her face.
 c being too friendly with people.
 d hair style.

4 'I must look just simply a wreck' (25,17) describes

 a the girl's eyes.
 b her tired appearance.
 c how she looks at her boyfriend.
 d the state of her clothes.

II

Fill in the correct preposition from the list below:

in, for, of, about, on, to, through, by, at, in, with

1 Go easy . . . the sugar, he said.
2 He was sitting . . . his desk all evening.
3 I'll meet you . . . the bus stop, she said.
4 I have ordered some cream . . . your coffee.
5 Do you like milk . . . your tea?
6 I'll put you . . . the bus, he told her.
7 He told the girl all . . . the party the night before.
8 He always went to work . . . train.

III

After reading the whole story, answer these questions:

1 How long had the girl been waiting at the table for the young man to arrive?
2 What was the young man's occupation?
3 Who did he say had thrown a party the night before?
4 What did the girl say she had been doing the night before?
5 What was it the girl said made her sick?
6 Who was the young man going to call up after the girl left him?
7 What was the girl going to do that evening?
8 What colour were the tables in the tea-room?

Discussion

The girl

1 How does the girl react when the young man arrives late?
2 In what way does she try to hide her real feelings when he tells her how wonderful Carol is?
3 Why does she keep on talking about Wally? Do you think she is really interested in him? Why does she tell the young man about all the people who want to take her out to tea?
4 What are the girl's views on liquor?

The boy

5 Describe the boy – his appearance, his character, his main interests.
6 What is his attitude to the girl? Is he fond of her or not? How can you tell?
7 What is his attitude to girls in general?
8 What are the main differences between the young man and the girl?
9 Why is the story called **The Last Tea**?

Written Work

Write an entry for the girl's diary describing her feelings in the tea-room and what had happened there.

OR

Write a letter from the young man to his best friend telling him about meeting Carol and about meeting the other girl in the tea-room next day.

General Discussion

This story tells us quite a lot about the way young people mix with each other in America; the 'dating' system, parties, dancing. What are your own views on dating?

Grammar Points

I What! in exclamations

What a night! (24,22)
What a looker she is! (24,30)
What a couple of eyes she's got! (25,4)

Change the following sentences into exclamations, using *What!*:

1 She wore lovely clothes. *What lovely . . .!*
2 He was a handsome young man.
3 There were a lot of old ladies in the tea-room.
4 She had beautiful blue eyes.
5 The girl had had a nice cup of tea.

II Used to/usually + verb

used to + verb (was/were in the habit of) = imperfect tense

She says she used to go to school with you. (25,7)
I used to just laugh at him. (25,32)

usually + verb (am, is, are/in the habit of) = present tense
(has/have been in the habit of) = perfect tense

She usually goes to school by bus.
I have usually been away at Christmas.

Change the following sentences by using *used to* or *usually* + *verb*

1 He is in the habit of swimming before breakfast.
2 They were in the habit of drinking a lot.
3 She has been in the habit of telephoning in the afternoon.
4 We were in the habit of meeting at the tea-room on Saturdays.
5 I am not in the habit of speaking to strangers.

Words and Phrases

I

I simply went ahead and ordered: I ordered without waiting for you. (24,5)
I was dying for a cup of tea: I was longing for a cup of tea. (24,5)
easy on the sugar: don't use so much sugar. (24,7)
Whadda matter?: what is the matter? (24,9)
I'm in terrible shape: I'm not feeling at all well. (24,10)
Was it feeling mizzable?: were you feeling miserable? (24,11) *it:* you
I'm all shot: I'm feeling terrible. (24,16)
I'm through: I'm finished. (24,20)
I'm off the stuff: I've given up drinking alcohol. (24,21)
it gave me the jumps: it made me feel nervous. (24,25)
she was throwing a party: she was giving a party. (24,26)
dame: slang for woman. (24,29)
a looker: a good-looking girl. (24,30)
public school: state-school, not privately run (in America). (25,9)
Can she step!: how she can dance! (25,12)
I must have been fried pretty: I must have been very drunk. (25,13)
influence: the power to get jobs for people. (25,31)
Garbo: Greta G., famous Swedish-born film actress in the 1930s. (25,32)
Keep your hair on: calm down, don't get so excited. (26,19)
crab about: shout about, be annoyed about. (26,21)
I was mean: I was unkind. (26,29)
I've got to fly: I must rush away. (26,38)
Solong: goodbye. (27,24)

II

There are a lot of words and phrases in this story which are peculiar to American English. Split up into groups and work through selected passages, noting down any words, phrases or spellings that are typically American. Then compare your results and see if you can draw any conclusions from them.

32

Enoch's Two Letters

Alan Sillitoe

Enoch's parents parted in a singular way. He was eight years of age at the time.

It happened one morning after he had gone to school, so that he didn't know anything about it till coming home in the evening.

5   Jack Boden got up as usual at seven o'clock, and his wife, who was Enoch's mother, set a breakfast of bacon and egg before him. They never said much, and spoke even less on this particular morning because both were solidly locked in their separate thoughts which, unknown to each other, they were at last intending to act on.

10   Instead of getting a bus to his foundry, Jack boarded one for the city centre. He sought out a public lavatory where, for the price of a penny, he was able to draw off his overalls, and emerge with them under his arm. They were wrapped in the brown paper which he had put into his pocket before leaving the house, a sly and unobtrusive movement as he called

15 from the scullery: 'So long, love. See you this afternoon.'

Now wearing a reasonable suit, he walked to the railway station. There he met René, who had in her two suitcases a few of his possessions that he had fed to her during clandestine meetings over the past fortnight. Having worked in the same factory, they had, as many others who were employed

20 there saw, 'fallen for each other'. René wasn't married, so there seemed nothing to stop her going away with him. And Jack's dull toothache of a conscience had, in the six months since knowing her, cured itself at last.

Yet they got on the train to London feeling somewhat alarmed at the

25 step they had taken, though neither liked to say anything in case the other should think they wanted to back out. Hardly a word was spoken the whole way. René wondered what her parents would say when they saw she'd gone. Jack thought mostly about Enoch, but he knew he'd be safe enough with his mother, and that she'd bring him up right. He would send

30 her a letter from London to explain that he had gone – in case she hadn't noticed it.

No sooner had Jack left for his normal daylight stint at the foundry than his wife, Edna, attended to Enoch. She watched him eat, standing by the mantelshelf for a good view of him during her stare. He looked up, half out of his sleep, and didn't smile back at her.

5   She kissed him, pushed sixpence into his pocket, and sent him up the street to school, then went upstairs to decide what things to take with her. It wasn't a hard choice, for though they had plenty of possessions, little of it was movable. So it turned out that two suitcases and a handbag held all she wanted.

10   There was ample time, and she went downstairs to more tea and a proper breakfast. They'd been married ten years, and for seven at least she'd had enough. The trouble with Jack was that he'd let nothing worry him. He was so trustworthy and easy-going he got on her nerves. He didn't even seem interested in other women, and the worst thing about

15 such a man was that he hardly ever noticed when you were upset. When he did, he accused you of upsetting him.

    There were so many things wrong, that now she was about to leave she couldn't bring them to mind, and this irritated her, and made her think that it had been even worse than it was, rather than the other way round.

20 As a couple they had given up tackling any differences between them by the human method of talking. It was as if the sight of each other struck them dumb. On first meeting, a dozen years ago, they had been unable to say much – which, in their mutual attraction, they had confused with love at first sight. And nowadays they didn't try to talk to each other about the

25 way they felt any more because neither of them thought it would do any good. Having come this far, the only thing left was to act. It wasn't that life was dull exactly, but they had nothing in common. If they had, maybe she could have put up with him, no matter how bad he was.

    For a week she'd been trying to write a letter, to be posted from where

30 she was going, but she couldn't get beyond: 'I'm leaving you for good, so stop bothering about me any more. Just look after Enoch, because I've had my bellyful and I'm off.' After re-reading it she put it back and clipped her handbag shut.

    Having decided to act after years of thinking about it, she was now

35 uncertain as to what she would do. A sister lived in Hull, so her first plan was to stay there till she found a job and a room. This was something to hang on to, and beyond it she didn't think. She'd just have to act again, and that was that. Once you started there was probably no stopping, she thought, not feeling too good about it now that the time had come.

34

An hour later she turned the clock to the wall, and walked out of the house for good, safe in knowing that shortly after Enoch came in from school his father would be home to feed him. They had lavished a lot of love on Enoch – she knew that – maybe too much, some of
5 which they should have given to each other but had grown too mean and shy to.

She left the door unlocked so that he could just walk in. He was an intelligent lad, who'd be able to turn on the gas fire if he felt cold. When Mrs Mackley called from her back door to ask if she was going on her
10 holidays, Edna laughed and said she was only off to see Jack's mother at Netherfield, to take some old rags that she needed to cut up and use for rug-clippings.

'Mam,' Enoch cried, going in by the back door. 'Mam, where's my tea?'

He'd come running down the road with a pocketful of marbles. His
15 head in fact looked like one of the more psychedelic ones, with a pale round face, a lick of brilliant ginger hair down over his forehead, and a streak of red toffee-stain across his mouth.

Gossiping again, he thought scornfully, seeing the kitchen empty. He threw his coat, still with the sleeves twisted, over to the settee. The house
20 did have more quiet than usual, he didn't know why. He turned the clock to face the right way, then went into the scullery and put the kettle on.

The tea wasn't like his mother made it. It was too weak. But it was hot, so he put a lot of sugar in to make up for it, then sat at the table to read a comic.
25 It was early spring, and as soon as it began to get dark he switched the light on and went to draw the curtains. One half came over easily, but the other only part of the way, leaving a foot-wide gap of dusk, like a long, open mouth going up instead of across. This bothered him for a while, until it got dark, when he decided to ignore it and switch the television on.
30 From hoping to see his mother, he began to wonder where his father was. If his mother had gone to Aunt Jenny's and missed the bus home, maybe his father at the foundry had had an accident and fallen into one of the moulds – from which it was impossible to get out alive, except as a skeleton.
35 Jam pot, butter dish, knife, and crumbs were spread over the kitchen table when he got himself something to eat. Not that it bothered him, that his father might have been killed, because when they had left him for an hour on his own a few months ago he had wondered what he would do if

35

they never came back. Before he'd had time to decide, though, they had opened the door to tell him to get a sandwich and be off to bed sharp, otherwise he'd be too tired to get up for school in the morning. So he knew they'd be back sooner than he expected. When Johnny Bootle's
5   father had been killed in a lorry last year he'd envied him, but Johnny Bootle himself hadn't liked it very much.

Whether they came back or not, it was nice being in the house on his own. He was boss of it, could mash another pot of tea if he felt like it, and keep the gas fire burning as long as he liked. The telly was flickering but
10   he didn't want to switch it off, even though heads kept rolling up and up, so that when he looked at it continually for half a minute it seemed as if they were going round in a circle. He turned to scoop a spoonful of raspberry jam from the pot, and swallow some more cold tea.

He sat in his father's chair by the fire, legs stretched across the rug, but
15   ready to jump at the click of the outdoor latch, and be back at the table before they could get into the room. His father wouldn't like him being in his chair, unless he were sitting on his knee. All he needed was a cigarette, and though he looked on the sideboard and along the shelf there were none in sight. He had to content himself with trying to whistle in a thick
20   manly style. Johnny Bootle had been lucky in his loss, because he'd had a sister.

If they didn't come back tonight he wouldn't go to school in the morning. They'd shout at him when they found out, but that didn't matter if they were dead. It was eight o'clock, and he wondered where they were.
25   They ought to be back by now and he began to regret that he'd hoped they never would be, as if God's punishment for thinking this might be that He'd never let them.

He yawned, and picked up the clock to wind it. That was what you did when you yawned after eight in the evening. If they didn't come soon he
30   would have to go upstairs to bed, but he thought he would get some coats and sleep on the sofa down here, with the gas fire shining bright, rather than venture to his bedroom alone. They'd really gone for a night out, and that was a fact. Maybe they were late coming back because they'd gone for a divorce. When the same thing had happened to Tom Brunt it was
35   because his mam had gone to fetch a baby, though he was taken into a neighbour's house next door before he'd been alone as long as this.

He looked along the shelf to see if he had missed a cigarette that he could put into his mouth and play at smoking with. He had good eyes and no need of glasses, that was true, because he'd been right first time. In

spite of the bread and jam he still felt hungry, and went into the scullery
for some cheese.

When the light went, taking the flickering telly with it, he found a torch
at the back of the dresser drawer, then looked for a shilling to put in the
5 meter. Fortunately the gas fire gave off enough pink glow for him to see
the borders of the room, especially when he shone the torch beam
continually around the walls as if it were a searchlight looking for enemy
planes.

   '*It was a long wait to Tipperary*' – as he had sometimes heard his father
10 sing while drunk, but his eyes closed, with the piece of cheese still in his
hands, and he hoped he would drop off before they came in so that they'd
be sorry for staying out so late, and wouldn't be able to be mad at him for
not having gone to bed.

   He walked across the room to the coat hooks in the recess, but his
15 mother's and father's coats had gone, as he should have known they
would be, since neither of them was in. There was nothing to put over
himself when he went to sleep, but he still wouldn't go upstairs for a
blanket. It would be as bad as going into a wood at night. He had run
across the road when a bus was coming, and seen Frankenstein once on
20 the telly, but he wouldn't go into a wood at night, even though lying
Jimmy Kemp claimed to have done so.

   Pushing one corner at a time, he got the table back against the
sideboard. There was an oval mirror above the mantelshelf, and he
leaned both elbows on it to get as good a look at himself as he could in the
25 wavering pink light – his round face and small ears, chin in shadow, and
eyes popping forward. He distorted his mouth with two fingers, and
curled a tongue hideously up to his nose to try and frighten himself away
from the bigger fear of the house that was threatening him with tears.

   It was hard to remember what they'd done at school today, and when
30 he tried to imagine his father walking into the house and switching on the
light it was difficult to make out his face very clearly. He hated him for
that, and hoped one day to kill him with an axe. Even his mother's face
wasn't easy to bring back, but he didn't want to kill her. He felt his knee
caps burning, being too close to the gas bars, so he stood away to let them
35 go cool.

   When he was busy rolling up the carpet in front of the fire, and being
away from the mirror, his parents suddenly appeared to him properly,
their faces side by side with absolute clarity, and he wished they'd come
back. If they did, and asked what the bloody hell he thought he was doing

rolling up the carpet, he'd say well what else do you expect me to do? I've got to use something for a blanket when I go to sleep on the settee, haven't I?

If there was one skill he was glad of, it was that he could tell the time.
5 He'd only learned it properly six months ago, so it had come just right. You didn't have to put a shilling in the clock, so that was still ticking at least, except that it made him feel tired.

He heaved at the settee, to swivel it round in front of the fire, a feat which convinced him that one day he'd be as strong as his father –
10 wherever he was. There was certainly no hope of the gas keeping on till the morning, so he turned it down to number two. Then he lay on the settee and pulled the carpet over him. It smelled of stone and pumice, and of soap that had gone bad.

He sniffed the cold air, and sensed there was daylight in it, though he
15 couldn't open his eyes. Weaving his hand as far as it would go, he felt that the gas fire had gone out, meaning that the cooking stove wouldn't work. He wondered why his eyelids were stuck together, then thought of chopping up a chair to make a blaze, but the grate was blocked by the gas fire. This disappointed him, because it would have been nice to lean over
20 it, warming himself as the bottom of the kettle got blacker and blacker till it boiled at the top.

When his eyes mysteriously opened, old Tinface the clock said it was half past seven. In any case there were no matches left to light anything. He went into the scullery to wash his face.
25 He had to be content with a cup of milk, and a spoon of sugar in it, with more bread and cheese. People were walking along the backyards on their way to work. If they've gone for good, he thought, I shall go to my grandma's, and I'll have to change schools because she lives at Netherfield, miles away.
30 His mother had given him sixpence for sweets the morning before, and he already had twopence, so he knew that this was enough to get him half fare to Netherfield.

That's all I can do, he thought, turning the clock to the wall, and wondering whether he ought to put the furniture right in case his parents
35 came in and got mad that it was all over the place, though he hoped they wouldn't care, since they'd left him all night on his own.

Apart from not wanting to spend the sixpence his mother had given him till she came back, he was sorry at having to go to his grandma's because now he wouldn't be able to go to school and tell his mates that he'd been all night in a house on his own.

He pushed a way to the upper deck of the bus, from which height he could look down on the roofs of cars, and see level into the top seats of other
5   buses passing them through the town. You never know, he thought, I might see 'em – going home to put a shilling each in the light and gas for me. He gave his money to the conductor.

It took a long time to get clear of traffic at Canning Circus, and he wished he'd packed up some bread and cheese before leaving the house.
10 Men were smoking foul fags all around, and a gang of boys going to Peoples' College made a big noise until the conductor told them to stop it or he'd put them off.

He knew the name of his grandmother's street, but not how to get there from the bus stop. A postman pointed the direction for him. Netherfield
15 was on the edge of Nottingham, and huge black cauliflower clouds with the sun locked inside came over on the wind from Colwick Woods.

When his grandmother opened the back door he was turning the handle of the old mangle outside. She told him to stop it, and then asked in a tone of surprise what had brought him there at that time of the
20 morning.

'Dad and Mam have gone,' he said.

'Gone?' she cried, pulling him into the scullery. 'What do you mean?' He saw the big coal fire, and smelled the remains of bacon that she must have done for Tom's breakfast – the last of her sons living there. His face
25 was distorted with pain. 'No,' she said, 'nay, you mustn't cry. Whatever's the matter for you to cry like that?'

The tea she poured was hot, strong, sweet, and he was sorry at having cried in front of her. 'All right, now?' she said, drawing back to watch him and see if it was.

30 He nodded. 'I slept on the couch.'

'The whole night! And where can they be?'

He saw she was worried. 'They had an accident,' he told her, pouring his tea into the saucer to cool it. She fried him an egg, and gave him some bread and butter.

35 'Our Jack's never had an accident,' she said grimly.

'If they're dead, grandma, can I live with you?'

'Aye, you can. But they're not, so you needn't worry your little eyes.'

'They must be,' he told her, feeling certain about it.

'We'll see,' she said. 'When I've cleaned up a bit, we'll go and find out what got into 'em.' He watched her sweeping the room, then stood in the doorway as she knelt down to scrub the scullery floor, a smell of cold water and pumice when she reached the doorstep. 'I've got to keep the place spotless,' she said with a laugh, standing up, 'or your Uncle Tom would leave home. He's bound to get married one day though, and that's a fact. His three brothers did, one of 'em being your daft father.'

She held his hand back to the bus stop. *If Uncle Tom does clear off it looks like she'll have me to look after.* It seemed years already since he'd last seen his mother and father, and he was growing to like the adventure of it, provided they didn't stay away too long. It was rare going twice across town in one day.

It started to rain, so they stood in a shop doorway to wait for the bus. There wasn't so many people on it this time, and they sat on the bottom deck because his grandma didn't feel like climbing all them steps. 'Did you lock the door behind you?'

'I forgot.'

'Let's hope nobody goes in.'

'There was no light left,' he said. 'Nor any gas, I was cold when I woke up.'

'I'm sure you was,' she said. 'But you're a big lad now. You should have gone to a neighbour's house. They'd have given you some tea. Mrs Upton would, I'm sure. Or Mrs Mackley.'

'I kept thinking *they'd* be back any minute.'

'You always have to go to the neighbours,' she told him, when they got off the bus and walked across Ilkeston Road. Her hand had warmed up now from the pumice and cold water. 'Don't kick your feet like that.'

If it happened again, he would take her advice. He hoped it wouldn't, though next time he'd sleep in his bed and not be frightened.

They walked down the yard, and in by the back door. Nothing was missing, he could have told anybody that, though he didn't speak. The empty house seemed dead, and he didn't like that. He couldn't stay on his own, so followed his grandmother upstairs and into every room, half expecting her to find them in some secret place he'd never known of.

The beds were made, and wardrobe doors closed. One of the windows was open a few inches, so she slammed it shut and locked it. 'Come on down. There's nowt up here.'

She put a shilling in the gas meter, and set a kettle on the stove. 'Might as well have a cup of tea while I think this one out. A bloody big one it is, as well.'

It was the first time he'd heard her swear, but then, he'd never seen her worried, either. It made him feel better. She thought about the front room, and he followed her.

'They kept the house clean, any road up,' she said, touching the curtains and chair covers. 'That's summat to be said for 'em. But it ain't everything.'

'It ain't,' he agreed, and saw two letters lying on the mat just inside the front door. He watched her broad back as she bent to pick them up, thinking now that they were both dead for sure.

Questions

The Author

Alan Sillitoe was born in Nottingham in 1928. His novels and short stories deal mainly with the lives of the industrial working classes. His first novel, *Saturday Night and Sunday Morning*, was published in 1958. More recent novels include *The Open Door* (1989) and *Last Loves* (1990). Sillitoe has also published seven collections of poetry.

The Story

Enoch's Two Letters is a story about a boy whose parents leave him – both on the same day. It is also a story about relationships; between a man and a woman, between parents and their child, between a child and his grandmother.

Points to Consider

While you read the story, think carefully about Enoch and the way he acts in every situation, also about his relationship with the different characters.

Listening Comprehension

Complete the sentences in the following (33,1–35,12):

1 When Jack left home that morning,

    a he got a bus to the foundry.
    b he called at a café and took off his overalls.
    c he went into the city centre.
    d he went for a walk in the country.

2 After Jack and René got on the train,

    a they were not very talkative.
    b they were both very happy about going to London.
    c Jack thought mostly about his wife Edna.
    d they talked a lot to each other.

3 When Jack had left the house,

    a Edna sat down to breakfast with Enoch.
    b Edna went up the street with Enoch.
    c Edna went upstairs and packed one suitcase.
    d Edna sent Enoch off to school.

4 Edna left the house intending

    a to return in a month.
    b to visit Jack's mother.
    c not to come back.
    d to stay away for a few days.

Reading Comprehension

I

Read the section 33,1–35,12 very carefully and then complete the following sentences in your own words:

1 When Jack came down at seven o'clock, . . .
2 Before leaving the house, Jack . . .
3 After saying goodbye to Enoch, Edna . . .
4 Edna was fed up with Jack because . . .
5 If it was cold when Enoch came home, he . . .

II

In the section 33,1–38,13 find

2 sentences that describe Jack's character.
2 sentences that describe Edna going to or from a place.
2 sentences that show how Enoch feels about the situation.
2 sentences that describe one of the characters' habits.

III

After reading the whole of the story, answer the following questions:

1 What did Enoch do with the clock when he first came into the house?
2 Whose chair did he sit on by the fire?
3 Where did he look, hoping to find a cigarette?
4 Why might his parents be mad at him when they came home?
5 How did he get the table against the sideboard?
6 What had Enoch learned to do only six months ago?
7 Why was he sorry at having to go to his grandma's?
8 What did the empty house seem like to Enoch?
9 Where did Enoch see the two letters?

Discussion

1 How did you enjoy the story? Did you find it interesting? Did you believe in the characters? What did you think of the way it started and ended? What was the story really about?
2 What kind of man is Jack? Does his wife really know him? What has she always thought about him?
3 Describe Edna. What sort of person is she? As a wife? As a mother?
4 Why did these two people decide to leave each other? What were their reasons? Were they valid reasons, do you think?
5 What does Enoch seem to think of his parents?
6 How do we realize that Enoch is still very much a child?
7 Describe Enoch's reaction when he thinks that his parents might have gone for good.
8 Why is the story called **Enoch's Two Letters**? Were the letters in fact written to Enoch?

Written Work

What might have happened next to Enoch, Edna and Jack? Write a continuation of the story.

OR

Write the letters that were written by Jack and Edna to each other. Imagine that you are Enoch. Write a letter to your mother/father, telling them what you think of the situation.

Role-play

Divide up into pairs. Act the following scenes:

1 Jack meets René at the station and tells her what he did from the time he got up that morning. If you are acting the part of René, you must help Jack by asking him questions.
2 Edna arrives in Hull and tells her sister what she did from the time she got up that morning.
3 Enoch meets his best friend at school and tells him what happened.

General Discussion

Today in many countries, divorce is becoming more and more common. How can this affect children? Should parents stay together even if they do not get on, for the sake of the children? Or is it better for children not to live with parents who are always quarrelling?

Grammar Points

I Preposition + the -ing form

He didn't know anything about it till coming home. (33,3)
= He didn't know anything about it till he came home.

Now rewrite the following sentences using the preposition + -ing form construction.

1 Before he walked to the railway station, Jack went to the city centre.
2 Jack had fallen in love with René since he got to know her.
3 Edna left the house after she had packed her suitcases.
4 While she watched Enoch eat his breakfast, Edna thought about what she was going to do.

Jack didn't go to the foundry. He went to the city centre.
= Instead of going to the foundry, Jack went to the city centre.

Now put the following sentences together using the preposition given + -ing form of verb.

1 Edna re-read the letter. Then she put it back in her bag. *After* . . .
2 Enoch turned the clock to face the right way. He then went to put the kettle on. *Before* . . .

3 He leaned both elbows on the mantelshelf. He got a good look at himself in the mirror. *By . . .*
4 She came out into the yard. She was very surprised to see him. *On . . .*

II Irregular comparison of adjectives and adverbs

They spoke even less on this particular morning. (33,7)
It made her think that it had been even worse that it was. (34,18)
She was not feeling too good about it. (34,39)

Now put the correct form of the words in brackets in the following sentences:

1 The . . . thing Enoch could possibly think of was going into a wood at night. *(bad)*
2 He liked his father . . . of all his relatives. *(little)*
3 He felt even . . . when the light went off. *(bad)*
4 He was . . . frightened in the morning when it got light. *(little)*
5 Enoch liked raspberry jam . . . than any other kind. *(good)*

Words and Phrases

I

a reasonable suit: quite a good suit. (33,16)
he had fed to her . . . . : he had given to her one at a time. (33,17)
'fallen for each other': come to love each other. (33,20)
she couldn't bring them to mind: she couldn't remember them. (34,18)
no matter how bad he was: however bad he was. (34,28)
I've had my bellyful: I've had enough. (34,31)
Hull: large city and port on the River Humber in north-east England. (34, 35)
This was/something to hang on to: something to hope for. (34,36)
safe in knowing: happy because she knew. (35,2)
rug-clippings: pieces of old clothes, etc.,: cut up and used to make a rug for the floor. (35,12)
one of the more psychedelic ones: of an unusual appearance because of the odd combination of colours. (35,15)
mash another pot of tea: make, brew another pot of tea, (in the north of England). (36,8)
telly: television. (36,9)
the telly was flickering: the picture was unsteady. (36,9)
when the light went: when the light went out. (37,3)

meter: box which measures gas or electricity used in a household and into which one puts money at regular intervals. (37,5)

It was a long wait to Tipperary: the real words of the song are 'It's a long way to Tipperary'. (37,9)

drop off: go to sleep. (37,11)

Frankenstein: the Frankenstein monster was the main character in a very popular horror film. (37,19)

eyes popping forward: eyes very wide open. (37,26)

gas bars: long pieces of metal or fire-clay used in gas-fires. (37,34)

number two: low measure of gas used in gas-fire. (38,11)

Weaving his hand: feeling with his hand from side to side. (38,15)

half fare: what a child pays on buses or trains. (38,31)

the upper deck: upstairs on a bus with two floors (a double decker). (39,3)

see level: see without having to look up or down. (39,4)

People's Colleges: places for further education. (39,11)

cauliflower clouds: clouds with the shape of a cauliflower. (39,15)

find out what got into 'em: find out what has made them do whatever they have done. (40,1)

clear off: leave. (40,8)

II

Enoch's grandmother speaks with many touches of local dialect which the author has reproduced in the dialogue. See if you can spot these and discuss what you think they mean.

Laurie Colwin   Mr Parker

Mrs Parker died suddenly in October. She and Mr Parker lived in a
Victorian house next to ours, and Mr Parker was my piano teacher. He
commuted to Wall Street, where he was a securities analyst, but he had
studied at Juilliard and gave lessons on the side – for the pleasure of it,
5   not for money. His only students were me and the church organist, who
was learning technique on a double-keyboard harpischord Mr Parker had
built one spring.

Mrs Parker was known for her pastry; she and my mother were friends,
after a fashion. Every two months or so they spent a day together in the
10   kitchen baking butter cookies and cream puffs, or rolling out strudel
leaves. She was thin and wispy, and turned out her pastry with abstract
expertness. As a girl, she had had bright-red hair, which was now the
colour of old leaves. There was something smoky and autumnal about
her: she wore rust-coloured sweaters and heather-coloured skirts, and
15   kept dried weeds in ornamental jars and pressed flowers in frames. If you
borrowed a book from her, there were petal marks on the back pages. She
was tall, but she stooped as if she had spent a lifetime looking for
something she had dropped.

The word 'tragic' was mentioned in connection with her death. She and
20   Mr Parker were in the middle of their middle age, and neither of them had
ever been seriously ill. It was heart failure, and unexpected. My parents
went to see Mr Parker as soon as they got the news, since they took their
responsibilities as neighbours seriously, and two days later they took me
to pay a formal condolence call. It was Indian summer, and the house felt
25   closed in. They had used the fireplace during a recent cold spell, and the
living-room smelled faintly of ash. The only people from the community
were some neighbours, the minister and his wife, and the rabbi and his
wife and son. The Parkers were Episcopalian, but Mr Parker played the
organ in the synagogue on Saturday mornings and on High Holy Days.
30   There was a large urn of tea, and the last of Mrs Parker's strudel. On the
sofa were Mrs Parker's sisters, and a man who looked like Mr Parker ten

48

years younger leaned against the piano, which was closed. The conversation was hushed and stilted. On the way out, the rabbi's son tried to trip me, and I kicked him in return. We were adolescent enemies of a loving sort, and since we didn't know what else to do, we expressed our love in slaps and pinches and other mild attempts at grievous bodily harm.

I loved the Parkers' house. It was the last Victorian house on the block, and was shaped like a wedding cake. The living-room was round, and all the walls curved. The third floor was a tower, on top of which sat a weathervane. Every five years the house was painted chocolate brown, which faded gradually to the colour of weak tea. The front-hall window was a stained-glass picture of a fat Victorian baby holding a bunch of roses. The baby's face was puffy and neuter, and its eyes were that of an old man caught in a state of surprise. Its white dress was milky when the light shone through.

On Wednesday afternoons, Mr Parker came home on an early train, and I had my lesson. Mr Parker's teaching method never varied. He never scolded or corrected. The first fifteen minutes were devoted to a warm-up in which I could play anything I liked. Then Mr Parker played the lesson of the week. His playing was terrifically precise, but his eyes became dreamy and unfocused. Then I played the same lesson, and after that we worked on the difficult passages, but basically he wanted me to hear my mistakes. When we began a new piece, we played it part by part, taking turns, over and over.

After that, we sat in the solarium and discussed the next week's lesson. Mr Parker usually played a record and talked in detail about the composer, his life and times, and the form. With the exception of Mozart and Schubert, he liked Baroque music almost exclusively. The lesson of the week was always Bach, which Mr Parker felt taught elegance and precision. Mrs Parker used to leave us a tray of cookies and lemonade, cold in the summer and hot in the winter, with cinnamon sticks. When the cookies were gone, the lesson was over and I left, passing the Victorian child in the hallway.

In the days after the funeral, my mother took several casseroles over to Mr Parker and invited him to dinner a number of times. For several weeks he revolved between us, the minister, and the rabbi. Since neither of my parents cared much about music, except to hear my playing praised, the conversation at dinner was limited to the stock market and the blessings of country life.

In a few weeks, I got a note from Mr Parker enclosed in a thank-you note to my parents. It said that piano lessons would begin the following
5 Wednesday.

I went to the Parkers' after school. Everything was the same. I warmed up for fifteen minutes, Mr Parker played the lesson, and I repeated it. In the solarium were the usual cookies and lemonade.

'Are they good, these cookies?' Mr Parker asked.
10 I said they were.

'I made them yesterday,' he said. 'I've got to be my own baker now.'

Mr Parker's hair had once been blond, but was greying into the colour of straw. Both he and Mrs Parker seemed to have faded out of some bright time they once had lived in. He was very thin, as if the friction of living had burned
15 every unnecessary particle off him, but he was calm and cheery in the way you expect plump people to be. On teaching days, he always wore a blue cardigan, buttoned, and a striped tie. Both smelled faintly of tobacco. At the end of the lesson, he gave me a robin's egg he had found. The light was flickering through the bunch of roses in the window as I left.
20 When I got home, I found my mother in the kitchen, waiting and angry.

'Where were you?' she said.

'At my piano lesson.'

'What piano lesson?'

'You know what piano lesson. At Mr Parker's.'
25 'You didn't tell me you were going to a piano lesson,' she said.

'I always have a lesson on Wednesday.'

'I don't want you having lessons there now that Mrs Parker's gone,' She slung a roast into a pan.

I stomped off to my room and wrapped the robin's egg in a sweat sock.
30 My throat felt shrivelled and hot.

At dinner, my mother said to my father, 'I don't want Jane taking piano lessons from Mr Parker now that Mrs Parker's gone.'

'Why don't you want me to have lessons?' I said, close to shouting. 'There's no reason.'
35 'She can study with Mrs Murchison.' Mrs Murchison had been my first teacher. She was a fat, myopic woman who smelled of bacon grease and whose repertoire was confined to 'Little Classics for Children'. Her students were mostly under ten, and she kept an asthmatic chow who was often sick on the rug.

'I won't go to Mrs Murchison!' I shouted. 'I've outgrown her.'

'Let's be sensible about this,' said my father. 'Calm down, Janie.'

I stuck my fork into a potato to keep from crying and muttered melodramatically that I would hang myself before I'd go back to Mrs Murchison.

The lessons continued. At night I practised quietly, and from time to time my mother would look up and say, 'That's nice, dear.' Mr Parker had given me a Three-Part Invention, and I worked on it as if it were granite. It was the most complicated piece of music I had ever played, and I learned it with a sense of loss; since I didn't know when the axe would fall, I thought it might be the last piece of music I would ever learn from Mr Parker.

The lessons went on and nothing was said, but when I came home after them my mother and I faced each other with division and coldness. Mr Parker bought a kitten called Mildred to keep him company in the house. When we had our cookies and lemonade, Mildred got a saucer of milk.

At night, I was grilled by my mother as we washed the dishes. I found her sudden interest in the events of my day unnerving. She was systematic, beginning with my morning classes, ending in the afternoon. In the light of her intense focus, everything seemed wrong. Then she said, with arch sweetness, 'And how is Mr Parker, dear?'

'Fine.'

'And how are the lessons going?'

'Fine.'

'And how is the house now that Mrs Parker's gone?'

'It's the same. Mr Parker bought a kitten.' As I said it, I knew it was betrayal.

'What kind of kitten?'

'A sort of pink one.'

'What's it name?'

'It doesn't have one,' I said.

One night she said, 'Does Mr Parker drink?'

'He drinks lemonade.'

'I only asked because it must be so hard for him,' she said in an offended voice. 'He must be very sad.'

'He doesn't seem all that sad to me.' It was the wrong thing to say.

'I see,' she said, folding the dish-towel with elaborate care. 'You know how I feel about this, Jane. I don't want you alone in the house with him.'

51

'He's my *piano* teacher,' I was suddenly in tears, so I ran out of the kitchen and up to my room.

She followed me up, and sat on the edge of my bed while I sat at the desk, secretly crying on to the blotter.

5 'I only want what's best for you,' she said.

'If you want what's best for me, why don't you want me to have piano lessons?'

'I *do* want you to have piano lessons, but you're growing up and it doesn't look right for you to be in a house alone with a widowed man.'

10 'I think you're crazy.'

'I don't think you understand what I'm trying to say. You're not a little girl any more, Jane. There are privileges of childhood, and privileges of adulthood, and you're in the middle. It's difficult, I know.'

'You don't know. You're just trying to stop me from taking piano

15 lessons.'

She stood up. 'I'm trying to protect you,' she said. 'What if Mr Parker touched you? What would you do then?' She made the word 'touch' sound sinister.

'You're just being mean,' I said, and by this time I was crying openly. It

20 would have fixed things to throw my arms around her, but that meant losing, and this was war.

'We'll discuss it some other time,' she said, close to tears herself.

I worked on the Invention until my hands shook. When I came home, if the house was empty, I practised in a panic, and finally, it was almost

25 right. On Wednesday, I went to Mr Parker's and stood at the doorway, expecting something drastic and changed, but it was all the same. There were cookies and lemonade in the solarium. Mildred took a nap on my coat. My fifteen-minute warm-up was terrible; I made mistakes in the simplest parts, in things I knew by heart. Then Mr Parker played the

30 lesson of the week and I tried to memorize his phrasing exactly. Before my turn came, Mr Parker put the metronome on the floor and we watched Mildred trying to catch the arm.

I played it, and I knew it was right – I was playing music, not struggling with a lesson.

35 When I finished, Mr Parker grabbed me by the shoulders. 'That's perfect! Really perfect!' he said. 'A real breakthrough. These are the times that make teachers glad they teach.'

We had lemonade and cookies and listened to some Palestrina motets.

When I left, it was overcast, and the light was murky and green.

I walked home slowly, divided by dread and joy in equal parts. I had performed like an adult, and had been congratulated by an adult, but something had been closed off. I sat under a tree and cried like a baby. He had touched me after all.

Questions

The Author

Laurie Colwin (1944–1992) was born and lived in New York. Her novels include *Happy All the Time* (1978) and *A Big Storm Knocked It Over*, published posthumously in 1993. This story is taken from the collection *Dangerous French Mistress and Other Stories*.

The Story

Young people can sometimes find grown-ups' ideas rather difficult to accept or understand. In **Mr Parker,** the author shows us how a young girl can be put in a situation in which she has conflicting loyalties.

Points to Consider

While reading the story, think about the following:

(*a*) where do Jane's loyalties really lie – with Mr Parker, or with her mother and father?

(*b*) what kind of man is Mr Parker? Are Jane's mother's suspicions totally unfounded?

Listening Comprehension

True or false? (48,1–49,33)

1 Mrs Parker's pastry was thin and wispy.
2 Mrs Parker grew weeds in ornamental jars.
3 Mrs Parker had suffered for many years from heart failure.
4 The Parkers belonged to the local Methodist church.
5 Jane and the rabbi's son were very good friends of a sort.
6 The Parkers' house was painted every five years.
7 Mr Parker was always telling his pupils off.
8 Mr Parker disliked Baroque music.

Reading Comprehension

I

Read the text carefully and find

2 sentences that describe the Parkers' house.
2 sentences that describe Mr Parker's taste in music.
2 sentences that tell us about Mrs Parker's appearance.
2 sentences that tell us about Jane's piano lessons.

II

Choose the correct answer in the following:

1 Which of the following words means nearly the same as 'tragic'? (48,19)

  a triumphant.
  b comical.
  c drastic.
  d dreadful.
  e passionate.

2 Which of the words below would you associate with the sentence 'the living-room smelled faintly of ash'? (48,25)

  a the seaside.
  b a hayfield.
  c a forest.
  d tobacco leaf.
  e perfume.

3 Which of the phrases below best explains the sentence 'The conversation was hushed and stilted'? (49,1)

  a difficult to understand.
  b in loud tones.
  c noisy and excited.
  d quiet and formal.
  e with long periods of silence.

III

After reading the whole story, answer these questions:

  1 Where did Mr Parker commute to every day?
  2 What was Mrs Parker known for?

3 What was the colour of her hair when she was a child?
4 What was the cause of Mrs Parker's death?
5 What did Mr Parker usually do on Saturday mornings?
6 What did the Parkers' house look like?
7 How often was the house painted?
8 What colour was it painted?
9 What music did Mr Parker like best?
10 Why did Jane's mother want her to stop having piano lessons with Mr Parker?
11 What did Mr Parker buy to keep him company after his wife died?
12 What did Mr Parker drink?
13 How did Jane perform on the piano, at the end of the story?

Discussion

1 What do you know about Mr Parker? His work? His pleasures? His appearance?
2 What can you find out about Mrs Parker?
3 Jane is a very observant girl. Give some examples of her powers of observation. Show how she manages, in very few words, to sum up people, places and situations.
    How do we understand at the end of the story that Jane is still really a child?
4 What do you think of Jane's mother? Is she perhaps over-protecting her daughter? What would you have done if you had been Jane's mother?

Written Work

Read the description of the Parkers' house again carefully. Write a paragraph about a house that you have visited recently.

General Discussion

1 'There are privileges of childhood and privileges of adulthood.' (52,12) What does Jane's mother mean by this statement, do you think? Can you give some examples from everyday life of the privileges of childhood and the privileges of adulthood?

2 Split up into pairs and talk about your musical tastes – classical or pop. Do you play a musical instrument? Did you take music lessons? Did you practise every day?

Grammar Points

I Relative pronouns: who, whose, which, that

Put the suitable relative pronoun in the gaps below.

Mr Parker was a man . . . was very fond of music. He had a harpsichord . . . he had built himself and a piano on . . . Jane had lessons. Mrs Parker, his wife, was a pleasant woman . . . pastry was well known in the neighbourhood. The Parkers' house . . . was the last Victorian house on the block, was shaped like a wedding cake. The living-room, . . . walls were curved, was round. One of the things . . . Jane always remembered was a stained-glass window a Victorian baby . . . eyes were like an old man's.

II Want someone to do something

Mini-dialogue

A What do you want Mrs Parker to do?
B I want her to help me with the baking.

Divide up into pairs. One of you can choose people from list **A.** The other can choose a suitable answer from list **B.** Use the above pattern.

A	B
the doctor	take a nap on my coat
the teacher	make the patient well
Jane	play a piece of Bach
Mr Parker	teach me good English
Mildred, the kitten	practise her piano lesson

'. . . basically he wanted me to hear my mistakes'. (49,22)
'Why don't you want me to have lessons?' (50,33)

Answer the following questions using the prompts given in brackets with the construction *want someone to do something*.

1 Why did Jane's mother take casseroles to Mr Parker?
(he, eat properly)

2 Why did Mr Parker send Jane a note?
(she, begin piano lessons)
3 Why did the girl's parents mention Mrs Murchison?
(she, study with Mrs Murchison)
4 Why did the girl's mother grill her about the events of the day?
(she, talk about Mr Parker)
5 Why did Jane work on the Invention till her hands shook?
(Mr Parker, be pleased with her)

Words and Phrases

I

Wall Street: street in New York, centre of finance. (48,3)
securities analyst: person who investigates bonds, stocks and shares. (48,3)
Juilliard: famous college of music in New York City. (48,4)
cream puff: light flaky pastry filled with jam and cream. (48,10)
strudel: type of German or Austrian cake made with thin leaves of pastry and filled with apple, etc. (48,10)
wispy: a little untidy, with bits of hair sticking out where they shouldn't. (48,11)
petal marks: marks where flowers had been pressed. (48,16)
condolence call: visit to tell Mr Parker how sorry they were about his wife's death. (48,24)
Indian summer: period of calm, dry weather in late autumn in the north of the USA. (48,24)
grievous bodily harm: phrase used in law to mean hurting someone very badly. (49,5)
the stock market: (the state of) the financial market. (50,1)
the friction of living: the damaging effects of everyday life. (50,14)
stomp: walk stiffly. (50,29)
sweat sock: thick sock used in running, gymnastics, etc. (50,29)
'Little Classics for Children': collection of simple piano music. (50,37)
melodramatically: with too much feeling. (51,4)
Invention: piece of music composed by J. S. Bach. (51,8)
grill: ask a lot of detailed questions. (51,17)
phrasing: way of expressing different passages in the music. (52,30)
motet: unaccompanied piece of music for many voices. (52,38)

II

In this story there are many words and phrases which describe people's appearances. Make a list of as many as you can for each of the characters.

A Member of the Family

Muriel Spark

'You must,' said Richard suddenly, one day in November, 'come and
meet my mother.'

Trudy, who had been waiting a long time for this invitation, after all was
amazed.

5 'I should like you,' said Richard, 'to meet my mother. She's looking
forward to it.'

'Oh, does she know about me?'

'Rather,' Richard said.

'Oh!'

10 'No need to be nervous,' Richard said. 'She's awfully sweet.'

'Oh, I'm sure she is. Yes, of course, I'd love—'

'Come to tea on Sunday,' he said.

They had met the previous June in a lake town in Southern Austria.
Trudy had gone with a young woman who had a bed-sitting-room in
15 Kensington just below Trudy's room. This young woman could speak
German, whereas Trudy couldn't.

Bleilach was one of the cheaper lake towns; in fact, cheaper was a way
of putting it: it was cheap.

'Gwen, I didn't realize it ever rained here,' Trudy said on their third
20 day. 'It's all rather like Wales,' she said, standing by the closed double
windows of their room regarding the downpour and imagining the
mountains which indeed were there, but invisible.

'You said that yesterday,' Gwen said, 'and it was quite fine yesterday.
Yesterday you said it was like Wales.'

25 'Well, it rained a bit yesterday.'

'But the sun was shining when you said it was like Wales.'

'Well, so it is.'

'On a much larger scale, I should say,' Gwen said.

'I didn't realize it would be so wet.' Then Trudy could almost hear
30 Gwen counting twenty.

59

'You have to take your chance,' Gwen said. 'This is an unfortunate summer.'

The pelting of the rain increased as if in confirmation.

Trudy thought, I'd better shut up. But suicidally: 'Wouldn't it be better
5   if we moved to a slightly more expensive place?' she said.

'The rain falls on the expensive places too. It falls on the just and the unjust alike.'

Gwen was thirty-five, a schoolteacher. She wore her hair and her clothes and her bit of lipstick in such a way that, standing by the window
10 looking out at the rain, it occurred to Trudy like a revelation that Gwen had given up all thoughts of marriage. 'On the just and the unjust alike,' said Gwen, turning her maddening imperturbable eyes upon Trudy, as if to say, you are the unjust and I'm the just.

Next day was fine. They swam in the lake. They sat drinking apple juice
15 under the red and yellow awnings on the terrace of their guesthouse and gazed at the innocent smiling mountain. They paraded – Gwen in her navy-blue shorts and Trudy in her puffy sun-suit – along the lake-side where marched also the lean brown camping youths from all over the globe, the fat print-frocked mothers and double-chinned fathers from
20 Germany followed by their blonde sedate young, and the English women with their perms.

'There aren't any men about,' Trudy said.

'There are hundreds of men,' Gwen said, in a voice which meant, whatever do you mean?

25 'I really must try out my phrase-book,' Trudy said, for she had the feeling that if she were independent of Gwen as interpreter she might, as she expressed it to herself, have more of a chance.

'You might have more of a chance of meeting someone interesting that way,' Gwen said, for their close confinement by the rain had seemed to
30 make her psychic, and she was continually putting Trudy's thoughts into words.

'Oh, I'm not here for that. I only wanted a rest, as I told you. I'm not—'

'Goodness, Richard!'

Gwen was actually speaking English to a man who was not apparently
35 accompanied by a wife or aunt or sister.

He kissed Gwen on the cheek. She laughed and so did he. 'Well, well,' he said. He was not much taller than Gwen. He had dark crinkly hair and a small moustache of a light brown. He wore bathing trunks and his large chest was impressively bronze. 'What brings you here?' he said to Gwen, looking meanwhile at Trudy.

He was staying at an hotel on the other side of the lake. Each day for the rest of the fortnight he rowed over to meet them at ten in the morning, sometimes spending the whole day with them. Trudy was charmed, she could hardly believe in Gwen's friendly indifference to him, notwithstanding he was a teacher at the same grammar school as Gwen, who therefore saw him every day.

Every time he met them he kissed Gwen on the cheek.

'You seem to be on very good terms with him,' Trudy said.

'Oh. Richard's an old friend. I've known him for years.'

The second week, Gwen went off on various expeditions of her own and left them together.

'This is quite a connoisseur's place,' Richard informed Trudy, and he pointed out why, and in what choice way, it was so, and Trudy, charmed, saw in the peeling pastel stucco of the little town, the unnecessary floral balconies, the bulbous Slovene spires, something special after all. She felt she saw, through his eyes, a precious rightness in the women with their grey skirts and well-filled blouses who trod beside their husbands and their clean children.

'Are they all Austrians?' Trudy asked.

'No, some of them are German and French. But this place attracts the same type.'

Richard's eyes rested with appreciation on the young noisy campers whose tents were pitched in the lake-side field. The campers were long-limbed and animal, brightly and briefly dressed. They romped like galvanized goats, yet looked surprisingly virtuous.

'What are they saying to each other?' She enquired of Richard when a group of them passed by, shouting some words and laughing at each other through glistening red lips and very white teeth.

'They are talking about their fast M.G. racing cars.'

'Oh, have they got racing cars?'

'No, the racing cars they are talking about don't exist. Sometimes they talk about their film contracts which don't exist. That's why they laugh.'

'Not much of a sense of humour, have they?'

'They are of mixed nationalities, so they have to limit their humour to jokes which everyone can understand, and so they talk about racing cars which aren't there.'

Trudy giggled a little, to show willing. Richard told her he was thirty-five, which she thought feasible. She volunteered that she was not

61

quite twenty-two. Whereupon Richard looked at her and looked away, and looked again and took her hand. For, as he told Gwen afterwards, this remarkable statement was almost an invitation to a love affair.

Their love affair began that afternoon, in a boat on the lake, when,
5   barefoot, they had a game of placing sole to sole, heel to heel. Trudy squealed, and leaned back hard, pressing her feet against Richard's.

She squealed at Gwen when they met in their room later on. 'I'm having a heavenly time with Richard. I do so much like an older man.'

Gwen sat on her bed and gave Trudy a look of wonder. Then she said,
10 'He's not much older than you.'

'I've knocked a bit off my age,' Trudy said. 'Do you mind not letting on?'

'How much have you knocked off?'

'Seven years.'

15 'Very courageous,' Gwen said.

'What do you mean?'

'That you are brave.'

'Don't you think you're being a bit nasty?'

'No. It takes courage to start again and again. That's all I mean. Some
20 women would find it boring.'

'Oh, I'm not an experienced girl at all,' Trudy said. 'Whatever made you think I was experienced?'

'It's true,' Gwen said, 'you show no signs of having profited by experience. Have you ever found it a successful tactic to remain
25 twenty-two?'

'I believe you're jealous,' Trudy said. 'One expects this sort of thing from most older women, but somehow I didn't expect it from you.'

'One is always learning,' Gwen said.

Trudy fingered her curls. 'Yes, I have got a lot to learn from life,' she
30 said, looking out of the window.

'God,' said Gwen, 'you haven't begun to believe that you're still twenty-two, have you?'

'Not quite twenty-two is how I put it to Richard,' Trudy said, 'and yes, I do feel it. That's my point. I don't feel a day older.'

The last day of their holidays Richard took Trudy rowing on the lake,
35 which reflected a grey low sky.

'It looks like Windermere today, doesn't it?' he said.

Trudy had not seen Windermere, but she said, yes it did, and gazed at him with shining twenty-two-year-old eyes.

'Sometimes this place,' he said, 'is very like Yorkshire, but only when the weather's bad. Or, over on the mountain side, Wales.'

'Exactly what I told Gwen,' Trudy said. 'I said Wales, I said, it's like 5 Wales.'

'Well, of course, there's quite a difference, really. It—'

'But Gwen simply squashed the idea. You see, she's an older woman, and being a schoolmistress – it's so much different when a man's a teacher – being a woman teacher, she feels she can treat me like a kid. I 10 suppose I must expect it.'

'Oh well—'

'How long have you known Gwen?'

'Several years,' he said. 'Gwen's all right, darling. A great friend of my mother, is Gwen. Quite a member of the family.'

15 Trudy wanted to move her lodgings in London but she was prevented from doing so by a desire to be near Gwen, who saw Richard daily at school, and who knew his mother so well. And therefore Gwen's experience of Richard filled in the gaps in his life which were unknown to Trudy and which intrigued her.

20 She would fling herself into Gwen's room. 'Gwen, what d'you think? There he was waiting outside the office and he drove me home, and he's calling for me at seven, and next weekend . . .'

Gwen frequently replied, 'You are out of breath. Have you got heart trouble?' – for Gwen's room was only on the first floor. And Trudy was 25 furious with Gwen on these occasions for seeming not to understand that the breathlessness was all part of her only being twenty-two, and excited by the boyfriend.

'I think Richard's so exciting,' Trudy said. 'It's difficult to believe I've only known him a month.'

30 'Has he invited you home to meet his mother?' Gwen enquired.

'No – not yet. Oh, do you think he will?'

'Yes, I think so. One day I'm sure he will.'

'Oh, do you mean it?' Trudy flung her arms girlishly round Gwen's impassive neck.

35 'When is your father coming up?' Gwen said.

'Not for ages, if at all. He can't leave Leicester just now, and he hates London.'

'You must get him to come and ask Richard what his intentions are. A young girl like you needs protection.'

63

'Gwen, don't be silly.'

Often Trudy would question Gwen about Richard and his mother. 'Are they well off? Is she a well-bred woman? What's the house like? How long have you known Richard? Why hasn't he married before? The
5   mother, is she—'

'Lucy is a marvel in her way,' Gwen said.

'Oh, do you call her Lucy? You must know her awfully well.'

'I'm quite,' said Gwen, 'a member of the family in my way.'

'Richard has often told me that. Do you go there *every* Sunday?'
10   'Most Sundays,' Gwen said. 'It is often very amusing, and one sometimes sees a fresh face.'

'Why,' Trudy said, as the summer passed and she had already been away for several weekends with Richard, 'doesn't he ask me to meet his mother? If my mother were alive and living in London I know I would
15   have asked him home to meet her.'

Trudy threw out hints to Richard. 'How I wish you could meet my father. You simply must come up to Leicester in the Christmas holidays and stay with him. He's rather tied up in Leicester and never leaves it. He's an insurance manager. The successful kind.'
20   'I can't very well leave Mother at Christmas,' Richard said, 'but I'd love to meet your father some other time.' His tan had worn off, and Trudy thought him more distinguished and at the same time more unattainable than ever.

'I think it only right,' Trudy said in her young young way, 'that one
25   should introduce the man one loves to one's parents' – for it was agreed between them that they were in love.

But still, by the end of October, Richard had not asked her to meet his mother.

'Does it matter all that much?' Gwen said.
30   'Well, it would be a definite step forward,' Trudy said. 'We can't go on being just friends like this. I'd like to know where I stand with him. After all, we're in love and we're both free. Do you know, I'm beginning to think he hasn't any serious intentions after all. But if he asked me to meet his mother it would be a sort of sign, wouldn't it?'
35   'It certainly would,' Gwen said.

'I don't even feel I can ring him up at home until I've met his mother. I'd feel shy of talking to her on the phone. I must meet her. It's becoming a sort of obsession.'

'It certainly is,' Gwen said. 'Why don't you just say to him, "I'd like

to meet your mother"'?'
'Well, Gwen, there are some things a girl can't say.'
'No, but a woman can.'
'Are you going on about my age again? I tell you, Gwen, I feel
5 twenty-two. I think twenty-two. I am twenty-two so far as Richard's
concerned. I don't think really you can help me much. After all, you
haven't been successful with men yourself, have you?'
'No,' Gwen said, 'I haven't. I've always been on the old side.'
'That's just my point. It doesn't get you anywhere to feel old and think
10 old. If you want to be successful with men you have to hang on to your
youth.'
'It wouldn't be worth it at the price,' Gwen said, 'to judge by the state
you're in.'
Trudy started to cry and ran to her room, presently returning to ask
15 Gwen questions about Richard's mother. She could rarely keep away
from Gwen when she was not out with Richard.
'What's his mother really like? Do you think I'd get on with her?'
'If you wish I'll take you to see his mother on Sunday.'
'No, no,' Trudy said. 'It's got to come from him if it has any meaning.
20 The invitation must come from Richard.'
Trudy had almost lost her confidence, and in fact had come to wonder if
Richard was getting tired of her, since he had less and less time to spare
for her, when unexpectedly and yet so inevitably, in November, he said,
'You must come and meet my mother.'
25 'Oh!' Trudy said.
'I should like you to meet my mother. She's looking forward to it.'
'Oh, does she know about me?'
'Rather.'
'Oh!'

30 'It's happened. Everything's all right,' Trudy said breathlessly.
'He has asked you home to meet his mother,' Gwen said without
looking up from the exercise book she was correcting.
'It's important to me, Gwen.'
'Yes, yes,' Gwen said.
35 'I'm going on Sunday afternoon,' Trudy said. 'Will you be there?'
'Not till supper time,' Gwen said. 'Don't worry.'
'He said, "I want you to meet Mother. I've told her all about you." '
'All about you?'

'That's what he said, and it means so much to me, Gwen. So much.'

Gwen said, 'It's a beginning.'

'Oh, it's the beginning of everything. I'm sure of that.'

Richard picked her up in his Singer at four on Sunday. He seemed
5 preoccupied. He did not, as usual, open the car door for her, but slid into
the driver's seat and waited for her to get in beside him. She fancied he
was perhaps nervous about her meeting his mother for the first time.

The house on Campion Hill was delightful. They must be very
comfortable, Trudy thought. Mrs Seeton was a tall, stooping woman, well
10 dressed and preserved, with thick steel-grey hair and large light eyes. 'I
hope you'll call me Lucy,' she said. 'Do you smoke?'

'I don't,' said Trudy.

'Helps the nerves,' said Mrs Seeton, 'when one is getting on in life. You
don't need to smoke yet awhile.'

15 'No,' Trudy said. 'What a lovely room, Mrs Seeton.'

'*Lucy,*' said Mrs Seeton.

'Lucy,' Trudy said, very shyly, and looked at Richard for support. But
he was drinking the last of his tea and looking out of the window as if to
see whether the sky had cleared.

20 'Richard has to go out for supper,' Mrs Seeton said, waving her
cigarette holder very prettily. 'Don't forget to watch the time, Richard.
But Trudy will stay to supper with me, I *hope*. Trudy and I have a lot to
talk about, I'm sure.' She looked at Trudy and very faintly, with no more
than a butterfly-flick, winked.

25 Trudy accepted the invitation with a conspiratorial nod and a slight
squirm in her chair. She looked at Richard to see if he would say where he
was going for supper, but he was gazing up at the top pane of the window,
his fingers tapping on the arm of the shining Old Windsor chair on which
he sat.

30 Richard left at half past six, very much more cheerful in his going than
he had been in his coming.

'Richard gets restless on a Sunday,' said his mother.

'Yes, so I've noticed,' Trudy said, so that there should be no mistake
about who had been occupying his recent Sundays.

35 'I dare say now you want to hear all about Richard,' said his mother in a
secretive whisper, although no one was in earshot. Mrs Seeton giggled
through her nose and raised her shoulders all the way up her long neck till
they almost touched her ear-rings.

Trudy vaguely copied her gesture. 'Oh yes,' she said, 'Mrs Seeton.'

'Lucy. You must call me Lucy, now, you know. I want you and me to be friends. I want you to feel like a member of the family. Would you like to see the house?'

She led the way upstairs and displayed her affluent bedroom, one wall of which was entirely covered by mirror, so that, for every photograph on her dressing-table of Richard and Richard's late father, there were virtually two photographs in the room.

'This is Richard on his pony, Lob. He adored Lob. We all adored Lob. Of course, we were in the country then. This is Richard with Nana. And this is Richard's father at the outbreak of war. What did you do in the war, dear?'

'I was at school,' Trudy said, quite truthfully.

'Oh, then you're a teacher, too?'

'No, I'm a secretary. I didn't leave school till after the war.'

Mrs Seeton said, looking at Trudy from two angles, 'Good gracious me, how deceiving. I thought you were about Richard's age, like Gwen. Gwen is such a dear. This is Richard as a graduate. Why he went into schoolmastering I don't know. Still, he's a very good master. Gwen always says so, quite definitely. Don't you adore Gwen?'

'Gwen is a good bit older than me,' Trudy said, being still upset on the subject of age.

'She ought to be here any moment. She usually comes for supper. Now I'll show you the other rooms and Richard's room.'

When they came to Richard's room his mother stood on the threshold and, with her finger to her lips for no apparent reason, swung the door open. Compared with the rest of the house this was a bleak, untidy, almost schoolboy's room. Richard's green pyjama trousers lay on the floor where he had stepped out of them. This was a sight familiar to Trudy from her several weekend excursions with Richard, of late months, to hotels up the Thames valley.

'So untidy,' said Richard's mother, shaking her head woefully. 'So untidy. One day, Trudy, dear, we must have a real chat.'

Gwen arrived presently, and made herself plainly at home by going straight into the kitchen to prepare a salad. Mrs Seeton carved slices of cold meat while Trudy stood and watched them both, listening to a conversation between them which indicated a long intimacy. Richard's mother seemed anxious to please Gwen.

'Expecting Grace tonight?' Gwen said.

'No, darling, I thought perhaps not *tonight*. Was I right?'

'Oh, of course, yes. Expecting Joanna?'

'Well, as it's Trudy's *first* visit, I thought perhaps not—'

'Would you,' Gwen said to Trudy, 'lay the table, my dear. Here are the knives and forks.'

Trudy bore these knives and forks into the dining-room with a sense of having been got rid of with a view to being talked about.

At supper, Mrs Seeton said, 'It seems a bit odd, there only being the three of us. We usually have such jolly Sunday suppers. Next week, Trudy, you must come and meet the whole crowd – musn't she, Gwen?'

'Oh yes,' Gwen said, 'Trudy must do that.'

Towards half past ten Richard's mother said, 'I doubt if Richard will be back in time to run you home. Naughty boy, I daren't think what he gets up to.'

On the way to the bus stop Gwen said, 'Are you happy now that you've met Lucy?'

'Yes, I think so. But I think Richard might have stayed. It would have been nice. I dare say he wanted me to get to know his mother by myself. But in fact I felt the need of his support.'

'Didn't you have a talk with Lucy?'

'Well yes, but not much really. Richard probably didn't realize you were coming to supper. Richard probably thought his mother and I could have a heart-to-heart—'

'I usually go to Lucy's on Sunday,' Gwen said.

'Why?'

'Well, she's a friend of mine. I know her ways. She amuses me.'

During the week Trudy saw Richard only once, for a quick drink.

'Exams,' he said. 'I'm rather busy, darling.'

'Exams in November? I thought they started in December.'

'Preparation for exams,' he said. 'Preliminaries. Lots of work.' He took her home, kissed her on the cheek and drove off.

She looked after the car, and for a moment hated his moustache. But she pulled herself together and, recalling her youthfulness, decided she was too young really to judge the fine shades and moods of a man like Richard.

He picked her up at four o'clock on Sunday.

'Mother's looking forward to seeing you,' he said. 'She hopes you will stay for supper.'

'You won't have to go out, will you, Richard?'

'Not tonight, no.'

But he did have to go out to keep an appointment of which his mother reminded him immediately after tea. He had smiled at his mother and said, 'Thanks.'

Trudy saw the photograph album, then she heard how Mrs Seeton had met Richard's father in Switzerland, and what Mrs Seeton had been wearing at the time.

At half past six the supper party arrived. These were three women, including Gwen. The one called Grace was quite pretty, with a bewildered air. The one called Iris was well over forty and rather loud in her manner.

'Where's Richard tonight, the old cad?' said Iris.

'How do I know?' said his mother. 'Who am I to ask?'

'Well, at least he's a hard worker during the week. A brilliant teacher,' said doe-eyed Grace.

'Middling as a schoolmaster,' Gwen said.

'Oh, Gwen! Look how long he's held down the job,' his mother said.

'I should think,' Grace said, 'he's wonderful with the boys.'

'Those Shakespearean productions at the end of the summer term are really magnificent,' Iris bawled. 'I'll hand him that, the old devil.'

'Magnificent,' said his mother. 'You must admit, Gwen—'

'Very middling performances,' Gwen said.

'I suppose you are right, but, after all, they are only schoolboys. You can't do much with untrained actors, Gwen,' said Mrs Seeton very sadly.

'I adore Richard,' Iris said, 'when he's in his busy, occupied mood. He's so—'

'Oh yes,' Grace said, 'Richard is wonderful when he's got a lot on his mind.'

'I know,' said his mother. 'There was one time when Richard had just started teaching – I must tell you this story – he . . .'

Before they left Mrs Seeton said to Trudy, 'You will come with Gwen next week, won't you? I want you to regard yourself as one of us. There are two other friends of Richard's I do want you to meet. Old friends.'

On the way to the bus Trudy said to Gwen, 'Don't you find it dull going to Mrs Seeton's every Sunday?'

'Well, yes, my dear young thing, and no. From time to time one sees a fresh face, and then it's quite amusing.'

'Doesn't Richard ever stay at home on Sunday evening?'

'No, I can't say he does. In fact, he's very often away for the whole weekend. As you know.'

'Who are these women?' Trudy said, stopping in the street.
'Oh, just old friends of Richard's.'
'Do they see him often?'
'Not now. They've become members of the family.'

Questions

The Author

Muriel Spark was born in 1918 and educated in Edinburgh. Her works include critical biographies of nineteenth-century writers, poetry and novels. Among her novels are *The Prime of Miss Jean Brodie* (1961), *The Mandelbaum Gate* (1965) and *Symposium* (1990).

The Story

A Member of the Family is about Trudy and Richard, who meet on holiday, but turn out to have rather different ideas about marriage.

Points to Consider

While reading the story, think about the following:

(*a*) details of appearance and dress.
(*b*) the contrast between Trudy and Gwen, the main women characters.
(*c*) the development of the relationship between Trudy and Richard.

Listening Comprehension

Complete the sentences in the following (59,1–60,35):

1 Trudy thought Southern Austria was like Wales because

  a it rained so much.
  b the sun shone so much.
  c it didn't rain much.
  d because the sun hardly ever shone.

2 Gwen acted as if

  a she wanted to find a husband.
  b she had stopped thinking about marriage.
  c she was very interested in Richard.
  d she was trying to stop Trudy from becoming interested in Richard.

3 Trudy wanted to try out her phrase-book alone because

    a she wanted to try out her German.
    b Gwen told her to do so.
    c she didn't want Gwen to hear her mistakes.
    d it might help her to meet a young man.

4 Gwen was speaking English to a man who was

    a accompanied by an aunt.
    b not accompanied by his wife.
    c accompanied by his brother.
    d accompanied by a sister.

Reading Comprehension

I

Read the section 59,1–63,14 carefully and find:

2 sentences that describe what people look like.
2 sentences that describe the weather.
2 sentences that show how any one of the characters feels about
    another.
2 sentences that describe Bleilach and its surroundings.

II

Choose the words from the list below which fit into the following
sentences:

confinement, crinkly, revelation, suicidal, virtuous, imperturbable,
appreciation, awning, indifference, invisible

1 It would be quite . . . to climb to the top of that mountain.
2 Trudy could not understand Gwen's . . . to Richard.
3 Gwen never seemed to worry about anything; she was quite . . . .
4 It was a . . . to Trudy when Richard showed her the town of Bleilach.
5 They sat under the . . . in the sun.

III

After reading the whole story, answer the following questions:

1 How old did Richard say he was?
2 Where were Trudy and Richard when their love affair began?
3 How many years had Trudy knocked off her age?
4 While Richard and Trudy were rowing on the lake, what did Richard say the lake looked like?
5 What was Gwen's occupation?
6 Where was Gwen's room?
7 What made Trudy think that Richard was getting tired of her?
8 Who took Trudy to the bus stop after she had left Richard's home?
9 Where had Richard's mother and father first met?
10 Name one of the other visitors Trudy met at Richard's home.
11 Who were these women visitors, according to Richard's mother?

Discussion

1 Give your first impressions of the story. What did you feel about the characters? What was the point of the title?
2 Where do Trudy and Richard first meet? Describe the place, Bleilach.
3 Describe Trudy. In what way does she change her personality when she meets Richard? Why does she lie to Richard about her age?
4 What part does Gwen play in the story?
5 Why does Trudy want Richard to ask her to meet his mother?
6 When he finally takes her to meet his mother, what does it mean for Richard?
7 What kind of woman is Richard's mother? How does she regard Richard?
8 What do you think of Richard's behaviour? Does anyone see Richard as he really is?
9 What would you have done at the end of the story if you had been Trudy?

Written Work

1 This story contains a number of detailed descriptions of people. Read them carefully, then find two photographs from a newspaper or magazine and give a description in detail of the people in them. Describe their height, build, clothes, hair, features and so on.
2 Write a postcard to a friend abroad describing briefly the town where you live. Notice the description of Bleilach in this story.

73

General Discussion

You have now read about Trudy's 'efforts' to get Richard to marry her.

1 How necessary is it for a girl to act like this today?
2 What are your views on marriage as an institution?
3 Discuss the roles of husband and wife within a marriage.

Grammar Points

I

They sat drinking apple-juice ... (60,14)
=They sat and drank apple-juice

Rewrite the following sentences using the pattern given:

1 Gwen and Trudy walked along the lakeside and looked at the other visitors.
2 It's just like Wales, said Trudy and turned to Gwen.
3 Richard kissed Trudy and looked into her eyes.
4 Trudy looked out of the window and fingered her curls.
5 The campers romped about and shouted to each other.

II Had better + verb

Trudy thought, I'd better shut up (60,4)

Practise using the phrase I'd/you'd/he'd, etc. better + verb by completing the following sentences, using the prompts below.

She, knock a bit off her age.
You, get up and get dressed.
They, learn some German.
We, stay indoors.
I, move to a more expensive place.

1 It's already 11 o'clock, so ...
2 It's pouring with rain, so ...
3 This hotel is awful, so ...
4 They can't understand a word the Austrians are saying, so ...
5 Richard likes younger women, so ...

III Do you mind + -ing

'I've knocked a bit off my age', Trudy said. 'Do you mind not letting on.' (62,11)

Complete the following sentences using the phrase 'Do you mind' + -ing form and the most suitable phrase from the list below.

Come with Gwen.
Go by bus.
Open the window.
Invite me to your home.
Help me to lay the table.

1 It's very hot in here . . .
2 I'd love to meet your mother . . .
3 I have such a lot to do . . .
4 Richard can't run you home tonight . . .
5 I'd like you to come here to supper next Sunday, too . . .

Words and Phrases

I

rather: of course, certainly. (59,8)

bed-sitting-room: one room used for sleeping, living and eating in. (59,14)

Kensington: part of West London where many older houses have been converted into bedsitter flats for single people. (59,15)

on a much larger scale: much bigger. (59,28)

counting twenty: count up to twenty to stop herself losing her temper. (59,30)

puffy: with a lot of material in it. (60,17)

close confinement: having been kept indoors together. (60,29)

a connoisseur's place: a place for people with good taste in art, architecture, etc. (61,13)

briefly dressed: with few clothes on. (61,25)

galvanized: suddenly active, as if forced, e.g. by an electric shock. (61,26)

M.G. racing car: very fast British sports car, made by the British Motor Corporation. (61,30)

show willing: try to please. (61,38)

volunteer: offer (information) without being asked. (61,39)

knock off: take off. (62,11)

let on: tell. (62,11)

experienced: knowing about love. (62,21)

Windermere: lake in the Lake District of north-western England. (62,37)

she would fling herself: she used to rush. (63,20)

he's calling for me: he's coming to fetch me. (63,21)

intentions: purpose with regard to Trudy (as far as marriage is concerned). (63,38)

well-bred: of a good family. (64,3)

a marvel: a wonderful person. (64,6)

young young: ironical, pretending to be very young. (64,24)

where I stand with him: what my position is. (64,31)

on the old side: rather old. (65,8)

Singer: make of sports car. (66,4)

comfortable: quite rich. (66,9)

Old Windsor chair: all wood chair with curved support for back and arms. (66,28)

run someone home: drive someone home by car. (68,12)

heart to heart (talk): talk as between very good friends. (68,22)

I'll hand him that: I must say that about him. (69,19)

II

'Trudy flung her arms girlishly round Gwen's neck' (63,33). Find other words or expressions which suggest that Trudy is trying to be younger than her age, and discuss them.

The Rain Came

Grace A. Ogot

The chief was still far from the gate when his daughter Oganda saw him. She ran to meet him. Breathlessly she asked her father, 'What is the news, great Chief? Everyone in the village is anxiously waiting to hear when it will rain.' Labong'o held out his hands for his daughter but he did not say a word. Puzzled by her father's cold attitude Oganda ran back to the village to warn the others that the chief was back.

The atmosphere in the village was tense and confused. Everyone moved aimlessly and fussed in the yard without actually doing any work. A young woman whispered to her co-wife, 'If they have not solved this rain business today, the chief will crack.' They had watched him getting thinner and thinner as the people kept on pestering him. 'Our cattle lie dying in the fields,' they reported. 'Soon it will be our children and then ourselves. Tell us what to do to save our lives, oh great Chief.' So the chief had daily pleaded with the Almighty through the ancestors to deliver them from their great distress.

Instead of calling the family together and giving them the news immediately, Labong'o went to his own hut, a sign that he was not to be disturbed. Having replaced the shutter, he sat in the dimly-lit hut to contemplate.

It was no longer a question of being the chief of hunger-stricken people that weighed Labong'o's heart. It was the life of his only daughter that was at stake. At the time when Oganda came to meet him, he saw the glittering chain shining around her waist. The prophecy was complete. 'It is Oganda, Oganda, my only daughter, who must die so young.' Labong'o burst into tears before finishing the sentence. The chief must not weep. Society had declared him the bravest of men. But Labong'o did not care any more. He assumed the position of a simple father and wept bitterly. He loved his people, the Luo, but what were the Luo for him without Oganda? Her life had brought a new life in Labong'o's world and he ruled better than he could remember. How would the spirit of the village survive his beautiful daughter? 'There are so many homes and so many

parents who have daughters. Why choose this one? She is all I have.'
Labong'o spoke as if the ancestors were there in the hut and he could see
them face to face. Perhaps they were there, warning him to remember his
promise on the day he was enthroned when he said aloud, before the
elders, 'I will lay down my life, if necessary, and the life of my household,
to save this tribe from the hands of the enemy.' 'Deny! Deny!' he could
hear the voice of his forefathers mocking him.

When Labong'o was made chief he was only a young man. Unlike his
father he ruled for many years with only one wife. But people mocked
him secretly because his only wife did not bear him a daughter. He
married a second, a third and a fourth wife. But they all gave birth to male
children. When Labong'o married a fifth wife she bore him a daughter.
They called her Oganda, meaning 'beans', because her skin was very
smooth. Out of Labong'o's twenty children, Oganda was the only girl.
Though she was the chief's favourite, her mother's co-wives swallowed
their jealous feelings and showered her with love. After all, they said,
Oganda was a girl whose days in the royal family were numbered. She
would soon marry at a tender age and leave the enviable position to
someone else.

Never in his life had he been faced with such an impossible decision.
Refusing to yield to the rain-maker's request would mean sacrificing the
whole tribe, putting the interests of the individual above those of the
society. More than that. It would mean disobeying the ancestors, and
most probably wiping the Luo people from the surface of the earth. On
the other hand, to let Oganda die as a ransom for the people would
permanently cripple Labong'o spiritually. He knew he would never be
the same chief again.

The words of Nditi, the medicine-man, still echoed in his ears. 'Podho,
the ancestor of the Luo, appeared to me in a dream last night and he asked
me to speak to the chief and the people,' Nditi had said to the gathering of
tribesmen. 'A young woman who has not known a man must die so that
the country may have rain. While Podho was still talking to me, I saw a
young woman standing at the lakeside, her hands raised above her head.
Her skin was as a tender young deer's. Her tall slender figure stood like a
lonely reed at the river bank. Her sleepy eyes wore a sad look like that of a
bereaved mother. She wore a gold ring on her left ear and a glittering
brass chain around her waist. As I still marvelled at the beauty of this
young woman, Podho told me, "Out of all the women in this land, we
have chosen this one. Let her offer herself a sacrifice to the lake monster!

And on that day, the rain will come down in torrents. Let everyone stay at home on that day, lest he be carried away by the floods." '

Outside there was a strange stillness, except for the thirsty birds that sang lazily on the dying trees. The blinding midday heat had forced the people into their huts. Not far away from the chief's hut two guards were snoring away quietly. Labong'o removed his crown and the large eagle-head that hung loosely on his shoulders. He left the hut and, instead of asking Nyabogo the messenger to beat the drum, he went straight and beat it himself. In no time the whole household had assembled under the *siala* tree where he usually addressed them. He told Oganda to wait a while in her grandmother's hut.

When Labong'o stood to address his household his voice was hoarse and tears choked him. He started to speak but words refused to leave his lips. His wives and sons knew there was danger, perhaps their enemies had declared war on them. Labong'o's eyes were red and they could see he had been weeping. At last he told them, 'One whom we love and treasure will be taken away from us. Oganda is to die.' Labong'o's voice was so faint that he could not hear it himself. But he continued, 'The ancestors have chosen her to be offered as a sacrifice to the lake monster in order that we may have rain.'

For a moment there was dead silence among the people. They were completely stunned; and as some confused murmur broke out Oganda's mother fainted and was carried off to her own hut. But the other people rejoiced. They danced around singing and chanting, 'Oganda is the lucky one to die for the people; if it is to save the people, let Oganda go.'

In her grandmother's hut Oganda wondered what the whole family was discussing about her that she could not hear. Her grandmother's hut was well away from the chief's court and much as she strained her ears, she could not hear what they were saying. 'It must be marriage,' she concluded. It was an accepted custom for the family to discuss their daughter's future marriage behind her back. A faint smile played on Oganda's lips as she thought of the several young men who swallowed saliva at the mere mention of her name.

There was Kech, the son of an elder in a neighbouring clan. Kech was very handsome. He had sweet, meek eyes and roaring laughter. He could make a wonderful father, Oganda thought. But they would not be a match. Kech was a bit too short to be her husband. It would humiliate her to have to look down at Kech each time she spoke to him. Then she thought of Dimo, the tall young man who had already distinguished

79

himself as a brave warrior and an outstanding wrestler. Dimo loved Oganda, but Oganda thought he would make a cruel husband, always quarrelling and ready to fight. No, she did not like him. Oganda fingered the glittering chain on her waist as she thought of Osinda. A long time ago
5   when she was quite young Osinda had given her that chain and, instead of wearing it around her neck several times, she wore it round her waist where it could permanently stay. She heard her heart pounding so loudly as she thought of him. She whispered, 'Let it be you they are discussing, Osinda the lovely one. Come now and take me away. . . .'
10   The lean figure in the doorway startled Oganda who was rapt in thought about the man she loved. 'You have frightened me, Grandma,' said Oganda laughing. 'Tell me, is it my marriage you were discussing? You can take it from me that I won't marry any of them.' A smile played on her lips again. She was coaxing her grandma to tell her quickly, to tell
15   her they were pleased with Osinda.
     In the open space outside the excited relatives were dancing and singing. They were coming to the hut now, each carrying a gift to put at Oganda's feet. As their singing got nearer Oganda was able to hear what they were saying: 'If it is to save the people, if it is to give us rain, let
20   Oganda go. Let Oganda die for her people and for her ancestors.' Was she mad to think that they were singing about her? How could she die? She found the lean figure of her grandmother barring the door. She could not get out. The look on her grandmother's face warned her that there was danger around the corner. 'Mother, it is not marriage then?' Oganda
25   asked urgently. She suddenly felt panicky, like a mouse cornered by a hungry cat. Forgetting that there was only one door in the hut, Oganda fought desperately to find another exit. She must fight for her life. But there was none.
     She closed her eyes, leapt like a wild tiger through the door, knocking
30   her grandmother flat to the ground. There outside in mourning garments Labong'o stood motionless, his hands folded at the back. He held his daughter's hand and led her away from the excited crowd to the little red-painted hut where her mother was resting. Here he broke the news officially to his daughter.
35   For a long time the three souls who loved one another dearly sat in darkness. It was no good speaking. And even if they tried, the words could not have come out. In the past they had been like three cooking-stones, sharing their burdens. Taking Oganda away from them would leave two useless stones which would not hold a cooking-pot.

80

News that the beautiful daughter of the chief was to be sacrificed to give the people rain spread across the country like wind. And at sunset the chief's village was full of relatives and friends who had come to congratulate Oganda. Many more were on their way, coming, carrying their gifts. They would dance till morning to keep her company. And in the morning they would prepare her a big farewell feast. All these relatives thought it a great honour to be selected by the spirits to die in order that the society might live. 'Oganda's name will always remain a living name among us,' they boasted.

Of course it was an honour, a great honour, for a woman's daughter to be chosen to die for the country. But what could the mother gain once her only daughter was blown away by the wind? There were so many other women in the land, why choose her daughter, her only child? Had human life any meaning at all? – other women had houses full of children while Oganda's mother had to lose her only child!

In the cloudless sky the moon shone brightly and the numerous stars glittered. The dancers of all age groups assembled to dance before Oganda, who sat close to her mother sobbing quietly. All these years she had been with her people she thought she understood them. But now she discovered that she was a stranger among them. If they really loved her as they had always professed, why were they not sympathetic? Why were they not making any attempt to save her? Did her people really understand what it felt like to die young? Unable to restrain her emotions any longer, she sobbed loudly as her age group got up to dance. They were young and beautiful and very soon they would marry and have their own children. They would have husbands to love and little huts for themselves. They would have reached maturity. Oganda touched the chain around her waist as she thought of Osinda. She wished Osinda were there too, among her friends. 'Perhaps he is ill,' she thought gravely. The chain comforted Oganda – she would die with it around her waist and wear it in the underground world.

In the morning a big feast of many different dishes was prepared for Oganda so that she could pick and choose. 'People don't eat after death,' they said. The food looked delicious but Oganda touched none of it. Let the happy people eat. She contented herself with sips of water from a little calabash.

The time for her departure was drawing near and each minute was precious. It was a day's journey to the lake. She was to walk all night, passing through the great forest. But nothing could touch her, not even

the denizens of the forest. She was already anointed with sacred oil. From the time Oganda received the sad news she had expected Osinda to appear any moment. But he was not there. A relative told her that Osinda was away on a private visit. Oganda realized that she would never see her
5 dear one again.

In the afternoon the whole village stood at the gate to say goodbye and to see her for the last time. Her mother wept on her neck for a long time. The great chief in a mourning skin came to the gate bare-footed and mingled with the people – a simple father in grief. He took off his wrist
10 bracelet and put it on his daughter's wrist, saying, 'You will always live among us. The spirit of our forefathers is with you.'

Tongue-tied and unbelieving, Oganda stood there before the people. She had nothing to say. She looked at her home once more. She could hear her heart beating so painfully within her. All her childhood plans
15 were coming to an end. She felt like a flower nipped in the bud never to enjoy the morning dew again. She looked at her weeping mother and whispered, 'Whenever you want to see me, always look at the sunset. I will be there.'

Oganda turned southwards to start her trek to the lake. Her parents,
20 relatives, friends and admirers stood at the gate and watched her go. Her beautiful, slender figure grew smaller and smaller till she mingled with the thin dry trees in the forest.

As Oganda walked the lonely path that wound its way in the wilderness, she sang a song and her own voice kept her company.

25   *'The ancestors have said Oganda must die;*
       The daughter of the chief must be sacrificed.
       When the lake monster feeds on my flesh,
       The people will have rain;
       Yes, the rain will come down in torrents.
30   *The wind will blow, the thunder will roar.*
       And the floods will wash away the sandy beaches
       When the daughter of the chief dies in the lake.
       My age-group has consented,
       My parents have consented,
35   *So have my friends and relatives;*
       Let Oganda die to give us rain.
       My age-group are young and ripe,
       Ripe for womanhood and motherhood;

But Oganda must die young,
Oganda must sleep with the ancestors.
Yes, rain will come down in torrents.'

The red rays of the setting sun embraced Oganda and she looked like a
burning candle in the wilderness.

The people who came to hear her sad song were touched by her beauty.
But they all said the same thing: 'If it is to save the people, if it is to give us
rain, then be not afraid. Your name will for ever live among us.'

At midnight Oganda was tired and weary. She could walk no more. She
sat under a big tree and, having sipped water from her calabash, she
rested her head on the tree trunk and slept.

When she woke up in the morning the sun was high in the sky. After
walking for many hours she reached the *tong*, a strip of land that
separated the inhabited part of the country from the sacred place – *kar
lamo*. No lay man could enter this place and come out alive – only those
who had direct contact with the spirits and the Almighty were allowed to
enter his holy of holies. But Oganda had to pass through this sacred land
on her way to the lake, which she had to reach at sunset.

A large crowd gathered to see her for the last time. Her voice was now
hoarse and painful but there was no need to worry any more. Soon she
would not have to sing. The crowd looked at Oganda sympathetically,
mumbling words she could not hear. But none of them pleaded for her
life. As Oganda opened the gate a child, a young child, broke loose from
the crowd and ran towards her. The child took a small ear-ring from her
sweaty hands and gave it to Oganda, saying, 'When you reach the world of
the dead, give this ear-ring to my sister. She died last week. She forgot this
ring.' Oganda, taken aback by this strange request, took the little ring and
handed her precious water and food to the child. She did not need them
now. Oganda did not know whether to laugh or cry. She had heard
mourners sending their love to their sweethearts, long dead, but this idea
of sending gifts was new to her.

Oganda held her breath as she crossed the barrier to enter the sacred
land. She looked appealingly at the crowd but there was no response.
Their minds were too preoccupied with their own survival. Rain was the
precious medicine they were longing for and the sooner Oganda could get
to her destination the better.

A strange feeling possessed the princess as she picked her way in the
sacred land. There were strange noises that often startled her and her first
reaction was to take to her heels. But she remembered that she had to

fulfil the wish of her people. She was exhausted, but the path was still winding. Then suddenly the path ended on sandy land. The water had retreated miles away from the shore, leaving a wide stretch of sand. Beyond this was the vast expanse of water.

5 Oganda felt afraid. She wanted to picture the size and shape of the monster, but fear would not let her. The people did not talk about it, nor did the crying children who were silenced at the mention of its name. The sun was still up but it was no longer hot. For a long time Oganda walked ankle-deep in the sand. She was exhausted and longed desperately for her
10 calabash of water. As she moved on she had a strange feeling that something was following her. Was it the monster? Her hair stood erect and a cold paralysing feeling ran along her spine. She looked behind, sideways and in front, but there was nothing except a cloud of dust.

Oganda began to hurry but the feeling did not leave her and her whole
15 body seemed to be bathing in its perspiration.

The sun was going down fast and the lake shore seemed to move along with it.

Oganda started to run. She must be at the lake before sunset. As she ran she heard a noise coming from behind. She looked back sharply and
20 something resembling a moving bush was frantically running after her. It was about to catch up with her.

Oganda ran with all her strength. She was now determined to throw herself into the water even before sunset. She did not look back but the creature was upon her. She made an effort to cry out, as in a nightmare,
25 but she could not hear her own voice. The creature caught up with Oganda. A strong hand grabbed her. But she fell flat on the sand and fainted.

When the lake breeze brought her back to consciousness a man was bending over her. 'O . . . . !' Oganda opened her mouth to speak, but she
30 had lost her voice. She swallowed a mouthful of water poured into her mouth by the stranger.

'Osinda, Osinda! Please let me die. Let me run, the sun is going down. Let me die. Let them have rain.'

Osinda fondled the glittering chain around Oganda's waist and wiped
35 tears from her face. 'We must escape quickly to an unknown land,' Osinda said urgently. 'We must run away from the wrath of the ancestors and the retaliation of the monster.'

'But the curse is upon me, Osinda, I am no good for you any more. And moreover the eyes of the ancestors will follow us everywhere and bad luck will befall us. Nor can we escape from the monster.'

Oganda broke loose, afraid to escape, but Osinda grabbed her hands again. 'Listen to me, Oganda! Listen! Here are two coats!' He then covered the whole of Oganda's body, except her eyes, with a leafy attire made from the twigs of *bwombwe*. 'These will protect us from the eyes of the ancestors and the wrath of the monster. Now let us run out of here.' He held Oganda's hand and they ran from the sacred land, avoiding the path that Oganda had followed.

The bush was thick and the long grass entangled their feet as they ran. Half-way through the sacred land they stopped and looked back. The sun was almost touching the surface of the water. They were frightened. They continued to run, now faster, to avoid the sinking sun.

'Have faith, Oganda – that thing will not reach us.'

When they reached the barrier and looked behind them, trembling, only a tip of the sun could be seen above the water's surface.

'It is gone! It is gone!' Oganda wept, hiding her face in her hands.

'Weep not, the daughter of the chief. Let us run, let us escape.'

There was a lightning flash in the distance. They looked up, frightened.

That night it rained in torrents as it had not done for a long, long time.

Questions

The Author

Grace Ogot was born in 1930 in central Nyanza, Kenya. She trained as
a nurse in Uganda and England and now lives in Kampala, Uganda.
She writes novels and short stories.

The Story

The Rain Came is about an African girl. It gives us a little insight into the
effects which tribal customs could have upon a family and their daughter.
It is a very moving story, and the author, who is herself from Kenya, has
captured for her readers the thoughts and feelings which for centuries
were common in tribal life.

Points to Consider

While reading the story, think about the following:

(*a*) the way Oganda's thoughts change as the story develops.
(*b*) where Labong'o's sympathies really lie.
(*c*) details which refer to tribal customs and tribal religion.

Listening Comprehension

True or False? (77,1–80,28),

1 Labong'o was very upset because his enemies had just declared war on
   him.
2 The people were sad when they heard that Oganda was to die.
3 It was customary for families like Oganda's to talk about the marriage
   of their daughters in their absence.
4 Oganda believed that Kech would make a suitable husband for her.
5 Oganda's relatives were dancing and singing in order to bring down the
   rain.

Reading Comprehension

I

Choose the correct answer to the following questions:

1 Which of the words below means almost the same as 'completely stunned'? (79,22)

    a bewildered.
    b excited.
    c bewitched.
    d unhappy.

2 Which of the alternatives below expresses the meaning of the phrase 'They would not be a good match'? (79,36).

    a They were not of the same age group.
    b They were physically unsuitable for each other.
    c They were intellectually unsuitable for each other.
    d They were not likely to share the same interests.

3 'They had been like three cooking-stones' (80,37) means

    a they had shared the same kitchen.
    b they had the same appearance.
    c they were dependent upon each other.
    d they always did the same kind of work.

4 Which of the following best agrees with the words 'they would have reached maturity'? (81,27).

    a They would have achieved their aim.
    b They would have grown old.
    c They would have become famous.
    d They would have reached adult life.

II

Choose from the text a word or phrase which means roughly the same as:

(a) mixed up, (b) make little of, (c) forefathers, (d) fortunate, (e) noisy, (f) tried hard to listen, (g) trapped.

III

After reading the whole story, answer the following questions:

1 Who was Oganda?
2 What was the atmosphere like in the village?
3 Who was Nditi?
4 Where was the young woman standing, in Nditi's dream?
5 What did the people do when they heard that Oganda must die?
6 What did Oganda think her family were discussing?
7 Name one thing Oganda did when she found out what the people were singing about.
8 What did Oganda's father give his daughter before she left him?
9 Where did Oganda say she would always be if her mother wanted to see her?
10 What did Oganda do as she walked towards the lake?
11 What did the small child run to give Oganda?
12 Why did Oganda's path end on sandy land?
13 Why did Oganda start to run when she saw the sun going down fast?
14 Who caught up with her as she ran?
15 What did her rescuer carry with him?
16 What did they see when they looked behind them from the barrier?

Discussion

1 Describe Chief Labong'o. Is he a good chief, do you think? Give your reasons. What is he like as a father?
2 How do the people react to the news that Oganda is to be sacrificed? Do you understand why they react like this?
3 What kind of girl is Oganda? Her appearance? Her character? How does she react to the news (*a*) at first? (*b*) later on?
4 Describe Oganda's feelings on the way to the lake. Is there anything to show that she questions what her forefathers have said she must do?
5 What kind of man do you think Osinda is? What is his attitude to old customs and traditions, do you think?
6 How does the story end? Is it a good ending? What do you suppose could have happened next?
7 Is this a very old story, or could it have happened in our time?

General Discussion

The family relationship in this story seems to be a close one. Compare and contrast it with family life in the city or community where you live.

Grammar Points

I As/like

On the other hand, to let Oganda die as a ransom for the people . . . (78,24)
She looked like a burning candle. (83,4)

Fill in the gaps in the following sentences:

1 . . . chief of the village, Labong'o had to do something for his people.
2 His daughter's skin was . . . the colour of the bean.
3 Oganda was greatly admired . . . the daughter of the chief.
4 She had to be offered . . . a sacrifice to the lake monster.
5 Oganda fought . . . a tiger to get out of the hut.
6 . . . all the other girls of her age group, Oganda wanted to marry and have children.

II Verb forms

Fill in the correct form of the verb in brackets:

1 The spirits had (*choose*) Oganda to (*lay*) down her life for the people.
2 She (*fight*) and tried to (*leap*) out of the hut.
3 Oganda's mother had (*bear*) only one child.
4 While Oganda (*lie*) on the sand, Osinda bent over her.
5 The chief had (*beat*) the drum to gather the people together.
6 The moon (*shine*) down and (*spread*) its light upon the dancers.
7 The chain Osinda had (*give*) her (*hang*) round her waist; she had (*wear*) it since she was quite young.
8 As she was (*lead*) away by the crowd, Oganda (*sing*) a sad song.

Words and Phrases

I

her co-wife: a woman with whom she shares her husband. (77,9)
crack: break down. (77,10)
shutter: door of hut. (77,18)
bean: plant bearing seeds in long pods; this bean, called Oganda in the Luo language, has a light golden colour. (78,13)
a tender age: a young age. (78,18)
siala tree: African tree used for timber and medicinal purposes. (79,10)
court: hut and surrounding area. (79,28)

the mere mention of her name: just the fact that her name was mentioned. (79,33)

soul: person. (80,35)

cooking-stone: stone used as support under cooking pot. (80,38)

burden: problem. (80,38)

pick and choose: eat exactly what she liked. (81,33)

tong: (Luo) borderland. (83,13)

kar lamo: (Luo) holy place. (83,14)

bwombwe: (Luo) climbing bush used by medicine man. (85,5)

bush: wild, uncultivated land full of bushes. (85,9)

II

In this story there are many words or phrases which refer to local African customs and/or beliefs, i.e. the ancestors, forefathers. Find other examples and discuss them.

The Valentine Generation

John Wain

Quarter to eight on a Monday morning, well into April but still pretty fresh, and I'm off to a fair start with the collecting. I may be getting on towards retiring age, but I can still get round the boxes as quick as any of them and quicker than most. The secret is to get a move on in the early
5   stages. Get round as many as you can by nine o'clock. After that, the traffic sets in heavy and slows you down so much that you can pretty well reckon to take double time over everything.

This morning I've got one of the light vans and it looks as if I'm getting away easy. I'm round the South-West Fifteen area, the other side of the
10 river. Nice quiet suburban streets, with trees in fresh bloom. Like a trip to the country. So of course I let myself be lulled into feeling optimistic. Forty years with the Post Office and I *still* haven't got it into my head that trouble always hits you when you've got your guard down.

I'm coming up to the third box and even as I drive up to it I can see this
15 girl standing there on the pavement. She's only a couple of yards away from the pillar-box, but my early warning system still doesn't go off: I think perhaps she's waiting for somebody to come out of one of the houses, some girlfriend she travels to work with or her little brother that she's seeing to school. Funny joke.
20 I get out of the van and go over to the box with my bunch of keys and my bag at the ready. And straight away I see that she's watching me. I try to take no notice, but her eyes are boring two holes in the back of my neck.

I open the box and there are the letters. Not many, because most people who post on a Sunday manage to catch the five o'clock collection.
25 About a couple of dozen in all. I'm just sweeping them into the bag when the girl takes a step towards me. I see her out of the corner of my eye and I straighten up. For a moment I wonder if I'm going to be coshed or something. There's a kind of desperation about her. But she's alone, a nice-looking girl, about twenty, good class, well dressed. She's very
30 unhappy, I can see that. All stirred up about something. But it's no business of mine. On the collecting, you've no time to spare before

nine o'clock. After that, you might just as well slacken off, that's what I always tell them.

I turn to go back to the van, but she's speaking to me. I don't quite catch what she's saying. She's too confused, the sounds just tumble out over one
5   another.

'Anything wrong, miss?' I say to her, but as I speak I'm opening the van door. She's not going to hold me up, whatever she wants.

'Yes,' she says. 'There's something terribly wrong. But you could put it right for me in a minute, if you'd be very kind.'
10   I don't like the sound of that, but she's waiting for me to say something, so I decide to give her one minute of my time. Just one minute. She's in trouble, and I've got daughters of my own.

'What is it I can do for you?' I say. 'It'd better be something I can do within sixty seconds, because on this job, it's all a question of how much
15   you can do before nine—'

She doesn't let me finish. She's all over me, reaching out as if she wants to grab hold of my arm. 'You can, you can easily do it straight away,' she says. 'It's just that – I've posted a letter that I ought never to have posted. And I want to get it back. If it goes it'll do terrible harm that I could never
20   do anything about. You will give it me, won't you? Please?'

It's a funny thing, but as I stand there listening to her I have a kind of 'This-is-where-I-came-in' feeling. All those years ago, when I first joined the Post Office, I used to wonder if anybody would ever come up to me when I was on collecting and ask me if they could have a letter back. And
25   now at last it's happened. Of course I've always known I couldn't do it.

'Sorry, miss,' I say, shaking my head. 'Firmest rule in the book. Once a thing's posted, it's in the care of the Post Office until it reaches the party it's addressed to.'

She draws a deep breath and I can see she's getting ready to work hard.
30   'Look,' she begins. But I'm too quick for her. 'No, you look,' I say to her. 'Forty years I've worked for the Post Office, and all through those forty years it's been my living. A job to do, a wage, pension at the end of it, social club, met most of my friends through it one way and another. It's like being married. Forty years and you don't even want a change. You
35   find you can't even imagine it any more.'

'Being married!' she says, gulping, as if I'd said something that really hurt her. 'I wouldn't know. I've never been married yet, and if you're going to stand on those regulations of yours and refuse to give just one little letter back, just *once* in forty years, I don't suppose I ever shall be.'

It's not that I'm heartless, but at that I just have to laugh. 'Oh, come *on*,' I say to her. 'A pretty young thing like you. Never married, that's a laugh!'

'Oh, you're so clever,' she says, sad and angry at the same time. 'You know everything, don't you? All right, probably if my entire happiness is ruined, I'll get over it one day, enough to marry somebody just for the sake of having a normal life and a family. But I shan't be happy.'

'We've all had it,' I say. 'Nobody in the world's good enough except just one person.'

'Don't you believe in love?' she asks.

'Well, as a matter of fact I do,' I say. 'I got married myself, soon after I joined the Post Office, and I can't believe I'd have been so happy with anyone else as I have with my wife. I did all right when I picked her out. But that was back in the days when marriages were made to last. Everything's different with you young people today.'

'You think so?' she says. 'Really different?'

'Course it is,' I say. 'All the romance has gone out of it. Well, look at it. Sex, sex, sex from morning to night and never a bit of sentiment.'

'What's wrong with sex?' she says, looking stubborn.

'Nothing,' I say, 'only in my day we didn't try to build a fire with nothing but kindling.'

I turn away, thinking I'll leave her to chew that one over. I'm just getting the van door open when suddenly she's there, grabbing at my wrist.

'Please,' she says. '*Please*. You've got a kind face. I know you'd help me if only you knew.'

'Well, I haven't got time to know,' I say, trying to get free. 'I thought you said it would be sixty seconds.'

'I wrote a letter to the man I'm in love with,' she says, speaking very quickly and holding on to my wrist. 'A horrible, hurtful letter telling him I didn't want any more to do with him, and saying a lot of horrible things that weren't even true. Things I just made up to try to hurt him – to make him suffer.'

'And now you're sorry for him,' I say. 'Well, write him another letter and tell him it was all a pack of lies.'

'You don't understand,' she says. 'It isn't that I'm sorry for him, it's just that I want him back. And he'll never, *never* come back to me if he reads that letter. He'll never forgive me.'

'He will if he loves you,' I say.

'Oh, it's hopeless,' she says with a kind of groan. 'You talk as if love was so simple.'

'Well, so it is,' I tell her. 'If two people love each other, they want to be nice, and help each other, and make things easy. I know there are lovers' quarrels, but they're soon patched up. Why, that's all part of the fun of being in love. You'll find out when the real thing comes along.'

'The real thing!' she groans again. 'I tell you this is the real thing, all the way through. Look, why don't you believe me and let me take my letter back?'

'I've told you why,' I say. 'Forty years with the Post Office and you want me to start ignoring regulations?'

'All right,' she says, speaking very low and looking at me fiercely. 'Go ahead and keep your regulations. But think about it sometimes in the middle of the night. How you sacrificed somebody's happiness for the whole of their life, rather than break a regulation.'

'I've told you before, you're being silly,' I say. 'Look, I'll prove it to you. Number one, you don't really love this bloke.'

'Don't love him!' she wails. 'How can you possibly tell that?'

'Well, does it look like it?' I say. 'You get your rag out about something, and straight away you write him such a stinking letter, full of insults and things that aren't even true, that you daren't go near him once he reads it.'

'That doesn't prove I don't love him,' she says. 'All it proves is that I was desperate. Look, let me tell you what happened.'

'All right,' I say, 'but make it fast. And don't kid yourself that I'll give you the letter when you've finished.' I meant it, too. Regulations mean a lot after forty years.

'I usually spend Saturday evening with Jocelyn,' she begins. *Jocelyn.* I don't like the sound of that. 'And last Saturday, that's the day before yesterday, he rings up and tells me he can't do it. He's got to look after his aunt who's coming up from the country. So when my brother and sister-in-law happened to look in and see me, I said I'd go out with them for the evening. We went up to the West End and I said I'd show them a nice little restaurant I know. So we went into this place and the very first person I saw was Jocelyn.'

'With his aunt from the country,' I say.

'With his aunt from the country,' she says, nodding and looking very grim. 'About twenty years old with a lot of red hair and a dress cut very low. And there was Jocelyn, leaning towards her the way he does when he's really interested in a girl.'

'What a surprise for him,' I say.

'No surprise,' she says. 'He never saw me. I knew at once I wouldn't be able to stand it. I wasn't going to have a show-down with him there and then, and as for sitting down and watching the performance and trying to eat my dinner, with my brother and his wife there on top of everything else, well.'

'So you ducked out quick, and came home and wrote him a nasty letter,' I say. Nine o'clock's creeping up and I'm ruddy nowhere with my collecting.

'If only I could have come straight home,' she says. 'But I have my brother and his wife to cope with. He's always saying I can't look after myself. I wasn't going to talk about it to him. So I looked round quickly and said sorry, this was the wrong place and I'd made a mistake. They said it looked all right and they'd like to try it anyway, but I said no, I was so keen to show them this special place. So there we were, out in the street, with them waiting for me to guide them and me with no idea where to go. We wandered about for ages, and my brother was in a filthy temper, and then I took them into a place and pretended that was it and it was awful. Oh, it was all so utterly, utterly awful I couldn't even talk. I could only say yes and no when they seemed to expect me to say something. I expect they thought I was mad.'

'So after *that* you wrote him a letter,' I say, trying to move her along even though the collections have now gone for a dead Burton.

'After that,' she says, 'I go home and spend a completely sleepless night. I don't even close my eyes, because every time I close them I see Jocelyn's face as he leans towards this girl.'

'All right, let him lean,' I say. 'If he's the type that runs after every bit of skirt he sees, he won't make you happy anyway.'

'But he *does* make me happy,' she says. 'He's absolutely ideal for me. He makes me feel marvellous. When I'm with him I'm really glad about being a woman.'

'Even if you can't trust him?' I ask.

'Casual infidelities don't matter,' she says. 'It's the really deep communication between a man and woman that matters.'

I can see this is getting out of my league altogether, so I make one more effort to brush her off. 'All right,' I say. 'If your Jocelyn is in the deep-communication business, he won't be put off by a nasty letter. He'll see straight away that you only wrote it because you were angry or desperate or whatever it is.'

'You're wrong,' she says, looking at me very steadily. 'There are some insults a man can't forgive. Listen, I wrote that letter on Sunday afternoon. I'd been crying nearly all morning, and every time I sat down to write I was just crying too much to see the paper. By the time I got
5   down to it I was feeling murderous. I wrote things that I knew he'd find absolutely unforgivable. I laughed at him, I told him he hadn't been adequate for me, that I'd had other lovers all the time we'd been together. I must have been mad. I wrote so many details he'll never believe it isn't true.'
10   'You say you love him?' I ask.
'I love him and need him utterly,' she says.
'Rubbish,' I say. The whole thing is beginning to get me down. 'If that's love, so is a boxing match. It's just vanity and sex, that's all it is. There's no love anywhere.'
15   'Well, perhaps that's not a bad definition,' she says, as if I've got all day to stand there and discuss it. 'I mean, one's need for another person is partly vanity isn't it? It's all bound up with one's own belief in oneself.'
'One this and one that,' I say. 'You're just hair-splitting. If you love
20   anybody, you care for them, don't you? You want them to be happy.'
'That's a chocolate-boxy idea of love,' she says. 'I mean it's not what happens when real people get involved with each other. You may have been able to live your life by those ideas, but in that case you've been very lucky. You've never had to face reality.'
25   Reality! From a chit of a girl like this I'm learning about reality!
'Oh, I'm sure you've had lots of reality in your life,' she says. 'I know you've had all sorts of responsibilities and everything. It's just that your personal relationships must have been unreal. You wouldn't talk about love in that sort of Royal Doulton way if they hadn't been.'
30   All at once I understood. She's not giving me her own opinions. She's just parroting what this Jocelyn's been teaching her. Deep communication between man and woman! I can just see his idea of it. Especially if he's got her trained so that she doesn't even count the other girls he runs after. And Royal Doulton! That's not the sort of thing she'd
35   think up for herself.
'Listen to me, miss,' I say. 'Take an old man's advice and leave that letter where it is. If it puts an end to this business between you and this Jocelyn bloke, believe me, you'll live to be grateful.'
At that she stares at me as if she's caught me doing something so

horrible she can't trust her own eyesight.

'It's unbelievable,' she says at last. 'If anybody had told me that – that ordinary human beings were capable of such stupidity and cruelty, yes, *cruelty*, I wouldn't have believed them.' And she begins to cry, quite
5   silently, with the tears running down her nose.

'Which of us is cruel?' I ask her. 'Me, or Jocelyn?'

'You, of course,' she says, so cross at what she thinks is cheek on my part that she stops crying. 'You're making me miserable *for ever* just so that you won't have to admit that your ideas about love are out of date
10   ·and wrong.'

'Whereas Jocelyn is sweetness and kindness itself, eh?' I put in.

'No, of course not,' she says. 'He's capable of hardness and aggressiveness and he can be cruel himself at times. That's all part of his being a real man, the sort of man who can make a girl feel good about
15   being feminine.' That's another bit of Jocelyn's patter, if I'm any judge.
'A man who was *sweetness and kindness itself,*' she goes on, bringing out the words as if they're choking her, 'wouldn't be capable of making a woman feel fulfilled and happy. He's got to have a streak of – of—'

'Of the jungle in him?' I say, trying to help her out.
20   'If you like, yes,' she says, nodding and looking solemn.

'Well, I don't like,' I say, letting it rip for once. 'I think you're a nice girl, but you're being very silly. You've let this Jocelyn stuff your head full of silly ideas, you've taken his word for it that he can chase every bit of skirt he meets, tell lies to you, string you along every inch of the way, and it all
25   doesn't matter because he's going to make you feel happy and relaxed, he's Tarzan of the flipping Apes. No, listen to me,' I tell her, because I can see she's trying to stick her oar in, 'I've stood here and listened to your story and made myself so late that the collections won't be right for the whole of today, and now I'm going to tell you what you ought to do.
30   You're a nice girl. Cut this Jocelyn out of your life like the rotten thing he is. Go and find some young man who'll tell you that as a woman you deserve to be cherished and taken care of. Who'll love you enough to tell you the truth and play fair with you. Even if he isn't an animal out of the Zoo. Make do with an ordinary human being,' I say to her. 'You'll find it
35   cheaper in the long run.'

Instead of answering, she just stands there crying. All right, I think to myself, let her get on with it. I've given her the right advice and that's the end.

I get into the van and press the self-starter. I'd left the engine running

but it doesn't idle fast enough on these crisp mornings, and it'd stalled. So anyway, I start it up and I'm just going to engage gear and move off when, for some reason, I can't do it. My foot comes off the accelerator and I look out of the window. There she is, still crying. Now's your cue to call me a
5 sentimental old fool.

So I get out of the van again and I go back to where she's standing, crying her eyes out.

'Look, miss,' I say, 'it's the best thing, you know. He wouldn't have been any good to you.'

10 'Why . . .' she begins, but she's crying too much to talk. I wait a bit and she has another go and this time it comes out. 'Why are you so sure that you know best and that I must be wrong?' she asks me.

'Well, it's simple,' I say. 'I've had a happy marriage for nearly forty years. So naturally I know how they work. I know what you have to do.'

15 'But love *changes*!' she says, bringing it out as if she's struggling for words that'll convince me. 'I'm sure you've been happy, but you're wrong if you think that your way of being happy would work for young people of today. You belong to a different generation.'

'And that makes me not human?' I ask. 'Look, I've been happy with
20 May for forty years and we've had three children. That's not done without love.'

'Your kind of love,' she says. 'Your generation's kind. I'll bet you used to send each other Valentines with sentimental rhymes on them.'

That gets my rag out. 'Yes, so we damn well did,' I say. 'And not only
25 that. We used to give one another keepsakes. Listen, the first time we ever went for a walk in the country, when we were courting, I picked some flowers for May and she took them home and pressed them between the leaves of a book – *and she's got them today!* Can you understand that? I wanted to love her and take care of her because she was a woman – that
30 was the way I made her feel good, not telling her a lot of stuff about deep communication and keeping one eye out for the next little piece that came in sight. Valentines!' I say, and I must be speaking quite loud, because some people on the other side of the road stop and stare at me, 'yes, we sent each other Valentines, big ones made of lace paper, shaped like
35 hearts, some of 'em. That's something else you wouldn't understand. Try talking to Jocelyn about hearts.'

That's done it. I've got carried away and now I'm as upset as she is. I'm ready to burst out crying myself. And me forty years with the Post Office. At this rate nobody'll get any letters at all.

'You think I don't know what love is, don't you?' the girl says. 'You're quite sure that whatever I feel for Jocelyn, it's not love.'

'Not what I'd call love,' I tell her. 'But you've got to excuse me. I don't know what love's supposed to be nowadays. I come from the wrong
5 generation.'

'The Valentine generation,' she says and all of a sudden she's smiling at me, yes, *smiling*.

'Weren't there women in your generation,' she says, 'who loved men and went on loving them even if they didn't treat them right? Didn't they
10 sometimes love husbands who got drunk or stayed away all night?'

'I've known the type,' I say.

'And what did you think about them?' she goes on. 'Did you think they were just fools who didn't know what they were doing?'

'That was different,' I say. 'A woman might go on loving a husband who
15 mistreated her. But at least she didn't say that she loved him *because* he mistreated her. She loved him in *spite* of it.'

'Are you sure?' she says. 'Was it always as clear as that just why she loved him?'

'What are you getting at?' I ask.

20 'I'm trying to get you to admit,' she says, 'that other people might know what love is besides you.'

'I'm quite sure they do,' I say. 'All I'm telling you is that you're wrong if you think you love this Jocelyn. You can't love a man who brings you so low.'

25 'And you're not even going to let me try,' she says, not crying now but just looking steadily into my face.

'Look,' I say, just to finish it. 'Let's have a bargain. You tell me what you think love is, and if I agree with you I'll give you your letter back.'

'Just that?' she says. 'Just tell you what I think love is?'

30 'Yes,' I say. I'm quite certain that whatever she says it'll be Jocelyn's angle.

'And you'll give me the letter back?' she says.

'If I agree with what you say, yes,' I say.

'Well,' she says, without even stopping to think, 'it's – wanting to be
35 with somebody all the time.'

'All the time? You're sure?' I ask her.

'It's wanting to wake up with the same person every morning and do everything together and tell each other everything,' she says.

'You know that, do you?' I say.

'Yes,' she says. 'I know that.'

I go over to the van and get the bag out. If anybody sees this, I can be sacked, forty years or no forty years. But there's hardly anybody about, and a bargain's a bargain.

5 'I'll be very quick,' she says, rummaging away. She shuffles the envelopes like a pack of cards and in no time at all she's found her letter and it's away, safe and sound, in her handbag.

'Bless you,' she says. 'I knew you'd want to help me really.'

'I did want to help you,' I say, ' and I still think I'd have helped you

10 more if I'd hung on to that letter.'

'Don't worry about me,' she says, smiling.

'Just tell me one thing,' I say as I'm opening the van door. 'Your idea of love. Would you say it was the same as Jocelyn's?'

'No,' she says, as chirpy as a sparrow. 'It's quite different.'

15 'What's going to happen, then,' I ask her, 'if you've both got different ideas about love?'

'I'll take care of that,' she says. I can see she's not worried at all. 'It's what I feel for him that matters, not what he feels for me. I just want him around, that's all.'

20 I get into the van and this time I drive away. The collections are up a big, tall gum tree. I have plenty of time stuck in traffic jams and I keep thinking of her and Jocelyn. How she doesn't care what he is or what he thinks or even what he *does,* so long as she has him. Doesn't sound like happiness to me. But all at once, the thought comes to me, well, she'll

25 probably get what she wants. I mean to say, it didn't take her long to get me to break a Post Office regulation I'd never broken in forty years. She twisted me round her little finger, so it could be she'll twist him.

But then, of course, I'm soft-hearted compared with a chap like that. The Valentine generation. I wonder what May'd say. Not that I'll ever

30 know. There are some things a man keeps to himself. 'Was she pretty?' I can hear her asking. 'Must have been, for you to stand there talking to her and get behind with your collections and finish up with risking the sack, and no provision for our old age.' No, the only way to get an idea would be to imagine May at that girl's age. She was a real woman. Not much Royal

35 Doulton there.

I wonder.

The Author

John Wain (1925–1994) was born in Stoke-on-Trent, Staffordshire. He worked as a university lecturer, literary critic, novelist and poet, becoming Oxford Professor of Poetry from 1973–78. His novels include *Hurry on Down* (1953), an amusing satire on life in post-war Britain and more recently, *Hungry Generations* (1994), a novel set in Oxford between the wars. This story is taken from the collection *Death of the Hind Legs* (1966).

Questions

The Story

The Valentine Generation is the story of a girl with a big problem on her mind, and a man who helps her to solve it at the risk of his job with the Post Office.

Points to Consider

While reading the story, think about the following:

(*a*) the way the girl uses all her feminine ways to try and make the postman help her.
(*b*) the unusual use of the present tense throughout the story.
(*c*) the many slang and colloquial expressions.

Listening Comprehension

Choose the correct answer in the following (91,1–92,20):

1 When the postman started his collection on Monday morning, it was

a 9.00 a.m.
b 7.45 a.m.
c 6.50 a.m.
d 8.45 a.m.

2 How long had the postman worked for the Post Office?

a For many years.
b For forty years.
c For twenty years.
d For ten years.

101

3 When the postman first saw the girl, she was

  a running towards him.
  b standing by her front door.
  c standing not far from the pillar box.
  d crossing the road.

4 The girl wanted her letter back because

  a she wanted to deliver it by hand.
  b she should not have sent it.
  c it was wrongly addressed.
  d she had not put enough stamps on it.

Reading Comprehension

I

After reading the whole story, answer the following questions:

1 How long had the postman been with the Post Office?
2 About how old was the nice-looking girl?
3 What was the rule of the Post Office about letters?
4 Why did the girl want her letter back?
5 What did the girl want the postman to believe about her?
6 What was her boyfriend's name?
7 Who did the girl see her boyfriend with in a restaurant?
8 Where did the girl go to after leaving the restaurant?
9 Who did she have with her?
10 When did she write her letter?
11 What did the postman say his wife's name was?
12 How many children had they?
13 What were their Valentines made of?

II

Complete the following sentences in your own words.

1 The postman was going to move off in his van . . .
2 The first time the postman ever went for a walk in the country with May . . .
3 The postman promised to return the girl's letter if . . .
4 The girl shuffled the envelopes quickly and . . .
5 The girl twisted the postman round her little finger, so he thought she . . .

III

Choose the correct alternative:

1 When the postman says the engine 'doesn't idle fast enough,' (98,1) he means

   a it takes a long time to warm up.
   b it doesn't run fast enough when it is standing still.
   c the engine is not capable of carrying a heavy load uphill.
   d it doesn't start quickly enough on cold mornings.

2 The girl told the postman he belonged to a different generation (98,18) because

   a he looked like a foreigner.
   b he was much older than she was.
   c he had had a happy marriage.
   d he belonged to a working-class family.

3 Why did the postman get 'carried away' and 'upset' (98,37)?

   a He was late with his collections.
   b He felt sorry for Jocelyn.
   c He was worrying about the post-office van.
   d He remembered his own courting days.

4 When the postman said 'There are some things a man keeps to himself' (100,30), he meant

   a he would never tell his workmates what had happened.
   b he would tell his wife quite a different story.
   c he would not tell the Post Office why he was behind with his collection.
   d he would say nothing to his wife about what had happened.

IV

Fill in the correct word in the following sentences from the list below:

chirpy, cue, bargain, stall, rummaging, courting, accelerator, sentimental, keepsake, convince, lace, idling, provision, admit

1 The man took his foot off the . . . and got out of the van.
2 Perhaps the girl thought he was a . . . fool.
3 What can I say that will . . . him?
4 The man watched her . . . away among all the letters.
5 Her husband gave her a . . . when they were . . . .
6 To settle the matter, they agreed to a . . . .

Discussion

1 How did you like the two characters, the postman and the girl? Do you like stories with an ending like this one? Or would you have ended it differently?
2 What kind of man is the postman? Try to describe him. Is he a good Post Office employee or not? What has he to lose if he gives in to the girl?
3 Describe the girl. Why has she written her letter and why does she now want it back? What kind of relationship does she have with Jocelyn?
4 At first, the postman and the girl seem to have very different ideas about love. How does the Valentine generation come into their conversation? What was different about that generation?
5 The postman and the girl make a bargain. What do you think of it?
6 How close, in the end, is the girl's idea of love to that of the postman? Is there any real difference between their two generations, after all?

Written Work

Imagine that the letter really went to Jocelyn after all. Try and write a further letter to Jocelyn explaining your feelings, as the postman suggests in 93,34.

General Discussion

1 *The generation gap*
People are always talking about the generation gap. What do they mean by it? Do you think it really exists? If so, can you think of any ways of bridging the gap?

2 *What is love?*
Comparing, for example, the relationship between the postman and his wife and the girl and Jocelyn, which comes closer to your personal idea of love?

Grammar Points

I The Simple and the Continuous forms of the verb.

When we were courting, I picked some flowers and she took them home and pressed them between the leaves of a book. (98,26)

104

I try to take no notice, but her eyes are boring two holes in the back of my neck. (91,21)

Revise the use of the Simple or Continuous forms of the verb, then use the correct form in the following. First do the exercises in the present tense, then in the past tense, for practice.

1 The postman *(get on)* towards retiring age.
2 As he *(drive up)* to the pillar box, he *(see)* the girl.
3 She *(stand)* by the pillar box as the van *(approach)*.
4 She *(say)* something to the postman, but he *(not understand)* what she *(say)*.
5 The girl *(try)* over and over again to make the postman give her back her letter, but he *(refuse)*.
6 Finally he *(promise)* to give it to her, but only if she *(tell)* him what she *(think)* love is.
7 While the girl *(look)* for her letter, the postman *(worry)* about his collections.
8 He *(have)* plenty of time to think about what has happened, while he *(wait)* in a traffic jam.

II Possessive pronouns

It's no business of mine. (91,30)
= It is not my business.

Rewrite the following sentences, using the pattern above.

1 He is one of my friends.
2 I found one of her letters.
3 Jocelyn was lunching with one of his aunts.
4 That is one of their old tricks.
5 I'm sure those were some of our photos.

Words and Phrases

I

well into: a long way into. (91,1)
be off to a fair start: start well. (91,2)
collecting: going round and picking up letters from all the post office pillar boxes. (91,2)
get a move on: hurry up. (91,4)
South-West Fifteen: district of London south-west of the Thames. (91,9)
early warning system: built-in ability to sense the danger. (91,16)
stand on: follow. (92,38)

get one's rag out: (slang) get very angry. (94,19)
stinking: unpleasant, nasty. (94,20)
kid oneself: believe falsely. (94,24)
the West End: part of London. (94,32)
cut very low: with a very low neckline. (94,37)
performance: what was happening. (95,4)
creep up: come nearer. (95,8)
ruddy nowhere: strong way of saying 'nowhere at all'. (95,8)
filthy: very bad. (95,17)
go for a dead Burton: be hopelessly delayed. (95,23)
a bit of skirt: (slang) girl. (95,27)
getting out of my league altogether: becoming too difficult. (95,35)
brush someone off: get rid of someone (95,36)
hair-splitting: making very small differences seem important. (96,19)
chocolate-boxy: unreal, too romantic, like the pretty picture on a chocolate box. (96,21)
Royal Doulton: fine English china. (here) Unreal, not very down-to-earth. (96,29)
patter: glib talk. (97,15)
let it rip: say exactly what one thinks. (97,21)
string someone along: have someone under control. (97,24)
Tarzan of the Apes: well-known film hero who lives in the jungle, is friendly with all the animals there, and does a lot of brave things. (97,26)
flipping: (slang) word without meaning, used to show strong feeling. (97,26)
stick one's oar in: interrupt. (97,27)
up a gum tree: (slang) lost, delayed. (100,21)

II

The postman uses many colloquial expressions, e.g. 'when you've got your guard down': when you are not prepared for something. Find other examples and put them into a non-colloquial form.

Martin Armstrong

The Rivals

The train was about three-quarters of an hour from its destination and was travelling at a good sixty miles an hour when Mr Harraby-Ribston, a prosperous businessman, rose from his seat, lifted his suitcase down from the rack and threw it out of the window. The only other occupant of the carriage, a small, thin man, a Mr Crowther, had raised his eyes from his book when his travelling-companion stirred from his seat and had noticed the occurrence. Then the two men exchanged a sharp glance and immediately Mr Crowther continued his reading, while Mr Harraby-Ribston resumed his seat and sat for a while puffing a little and with a heightened colour as a result of his exertion. The glance that his companion had given him worried him extremely, for Mr Crowther's glance had betrayed not the smallest emotion. It had shown no alarm, no surprise, not even a mild interest, and that, surely, was very extraordinary. Mr Harraby-Ribston's curiosity was violently aroused. And not only that. He was by nature a sociable, loquacious man and he had reckoned that his action would infallibly produce conversation. But no conversation had supervened and, that being so, he had had no opportunity of explaining his behaviour and he began to feel that he had merely made a fool of himself in the eyes of his companion, or, worse, that his companion might conclude that the suitcase contained a corpse, in which event he would perhaps inform the police when they reached their destination and all sorts of troublesome and humiliating enquiries would ensue. Such were the thoughts and conjectures that buzzed round Mr Harraby-Ribston, robbing him of the satisfaction and refreshment that were his due.

Mr Crowther, for his part, had also suffered some distraction. Though he was pretending to read, he was actually unable to do so. For all his appearance of apathy, the spectacle of a well-to-do gentleman pitching a suitcase from the window of a moving train had surprised him very much. But he had not betrayed his surprise. The fellow was obviously counting on him for a violent reaction and so Mr Crowther made a point of not

reacting. Whether the thing was a practical joke or not, Mr Crowther considered it as unwarrantable infringement of his privacy. It was as if the fellow had burst a paper bag in the hope of making him jump. Well, he wasn't going to jump, he wasn't going to pander to that sort of thing. If the
5   fellow imagined that to throw a suitcase out of the window gave him some sort of importance, well, he was mistaken.

But Mr Harraby-Ribston had reached a point at which he must either speak or burst and, preferring the former alternative, he said: 'Excuse me, sir, but I must say, you surprise me.'

10   Mr Crowther raised a languid eye from his book. 'Surprise you?' he said. 'Does reading in the train surprise you?'

'No, no!' said Mr Harraby-Ribston. 'I wasn't referring to that. What surprises me is that you weren't surprised when I threw my suitcase out of the window.'

15   'Indeed? That surprised you? You're very easily surprised.'

'I don't know about that. Surely, surely, my dear sir, it was, to say the least of it, an unusual sight. I dare bet you've never before seen a man throw a suitcase from the window of a moving train.'

Mr Crowther reflected. 'I don't know that I have; but then, to the best
20   of my recollection, I've never seen a man eat a raw turnip in the train or dance a Highland Fling during family prayers for that matter. But what of it? If one allowed oneself to be surprised at anything, however insignificant, one's whole life would consist of a series of trivial astonishments.'

25   'And you think it an insignificant act to throw one's suitcase out of a railway-carriage window?'

'Totally!' said Mr Crowther, and his eyes again sought his book.

'Then what, if I may ask,' said the other, evidently somewhat nettled, 'would you consider a significant act?'

30   Mr Crowther shrugged his shoulders wearily. 'Perhaps I would have thought it significant if the suitcase had been mine.'

'I see. You think yourself more important than me.'

'I am not aware,' said Mr Crowther, 'that I mentioned myself, but I certainly consider my suitcase more important than yours, and in saying
35   this I make no reference to the quality of the leather, but merely to the fact that I am myself, while you are a total stranger.'

'And the affairs of strangers don't interest you?'

'Only in so far as they impinge upon mine.'

'Well,' said Mr Harraby-Ribston, 'I should certainly have thought that when I threw my suitcase out of the window it could hardly have failed to impinge somewhat . . .'

'Not in the least!' said Mr Crowther coldly.

'It only shows,' Mr Harraby-Ribston remarked, 'how people differ. Now if you had thrown your suitcase out of the window, I should have been extremely curious to know why you did it.'

'I gather,' replied Mr Crowther with complete detachment, 'that you are anxious to tell me why *you* did it.'

'Not if it wouldn't interest you, though, I must say, I find it hard to believe that anyone could fail to be interested.'

He paused, but Mr Crowther made no reply; on the contrary, he showed every sign of resuming his reading. To forestall this, Mr Harraby-Ribston leaned back in his seat and launched out.

'The truth of the matter is that I have just, an hour and a half ago, abandoned home and wife and am starting life afresh, and the reason why I threw my suitcase out of the window just now was that I had suddenly realized that in it I was taking some of the old life with me. Clothes, hairbrushes and so on all have their associations, and associations are precisely what I want to be rid of. Hence my rather unusual action. I'm no chicken, I admit; I'm a man of nearly fifty, I've been married for twenty-one years, and yet here I am, starting life afresh. Well, that may seem to you a very extraordinary thing to do.'

'On the contrary,' said Mr Crowther, 'nothing could be more natural.'

Mr Harraby-Ribston was somewhat taken aback. 'Natural? You think it natural? I must say, you surprise me.'

'You seem to me,' said Mr Crowther, 'a man much given to surprise.'

'While you, I take it,' Mr Harraby-Ribston snapped back, 'pride yourself on being surprised by nothing.'

'Not at all!' replied Mr Crowther. 'The point is, I think, that we are surprised by different things. You tell me you've been married for twenty-one years and then expect me to be surprised when you add that you're now leaving your wife. But, my dear sir, I find nothing surprising about that. What does surprise me is that you've been so long in doing so.'

Mr Harraby-Ribston considered this view. 'I take it,' he said at last, 'that you're not, yourself, a married man.'

'Not now,' Mr Crowther replied.

'Not now? You mean you've been married and you've left your wife?'

'Not quite that. Leaving one's wife involves leaving one's home, and that was out of the question. I'm very fond of my home; a charming house, a charming garden, and doubly charming nowadays when I have them to myself.'

'You mean, then, that you turned your wife out?'

'O no, no! That would have involved all sorts of unpleasantness.'

5 'Then what,' asked Mr Harraby-Ribston, all curiosity once more, 'what did you do?'

The other waved his hand airily. 'There are other ways, simpler ways.'

'I should like to know them,' said Mr Harraby-Ribston.

'I don't think,' said Mr Crowther, 'that my particular method would be

10 quite in your line.'

'But why not?' Mr Harraby-Ribston was simply bubbling with curiosity.

'Why not? Well, my method requires . . . what shall I say? . . . reticence, tact, and a lot of very careful planning.'

15 'And you think I'm incapable of that?'

'Well,' said Mr Crowther, 'I should have said that reticence was not your strong point; and your evident desire to arouse surprise in others – that, if you were to adopt my method, might land you in a very uncomfortable position.'

20 'You interest me enormously,' said Mr Harraby-Ribston. 'Now do, please, just tell me what you did.'

Mr Crowther seemed to hesitate, then to make up his mind. 'If I tell you, I trust you won't accuse me of any wish to surprise you. I've never had the slightest desire to surprise anybody. Observe, please, that I

25 haven't forced the information on you. If you hadn't spoken to me, we should have travelled in complete silence. I have a book here which interests me greatly and if you hadn't, if I may say so, dragged me into conversation . . .'

'Quite! Quite!' said Mr Harraby-Ribston, who, by now, was worked up

30 to a dangerous pitch of excitement. 'I admit it; I admit it entirely. And I promise you I'll do my best not to appear in the least surprised.'

'Well,' said Mr Crowther, 'what I did was simply this. Forgive me if it seems to you a little sensational, and remember, please, that I shall deeply resent any appearance of astonishment on your part. Well, as I was

35 saying, I simply murdered my wife.'

Mr Harraby-Ribston took the disclosure remarkably well. He did, it's true, flinch and turn a little pale, but in a few moments he had recovered himself. 'Thank you, sir,' he said; and let me say how much I appreciate your openness. In fact you tempt me to be equally frank with you. Let me confess, then, that as a matter of fact I haven't left my wife, for the simple reason that I'm a bachelor. I grow vegetables on rather a large scale and once a week business takes me to London. As for the matter of the suitcase, I have some friends whose house we passed a few miles back, and every week I fill a suitcase (a very old suitcase, as you perhaps noticed) with vegetables, bring it with me, and throw it out of the carriage-window as the train passes their house. It rolls down the embankment and lands up against their railings. It's a primitive method, I know, but it saves postage and you can have no idea how much entertaining conversation it provokes with my fellow-passengers. You, if I may say so, are no exception.'

Questions

The Author

Martin Armstrong was born in Newcastle-upon-Tyne in 1882. After university studies he became a journalist and novelist. He has published two novels, *Lovers' Leap* and *Snakes in the Grass,* eight collections of short stories and poems. He died in 1974.

The Story

The Rivals is a story about two gentlemen who meet on a train. One of the gentlemen does a very unusual thing, which results in a strange conversation between them. There is a lot of so-called 'fencing' (that is, not being quite truthful), and a lot of rivalry, but in the end one man turns out to be as good, or as bad, you may think, as the other. Notice the rather literary style with a number of difficult words. By the end of the story, we hope you will be able to decide how suitable the title is!

Points to Consider

While reading the story, notice the way that the two characters calmly carry on their conversation. Make a note of any particularly colloquial phrases they use.

Listening Comprehension

Choose the correct answer in the following (107,1–108,24):

1 The other occupant of Mr Harraby-Ribston's compartment on the train was

  a a tall thin man.
  b a short fat man.
  c a big heavy man.
  d a small thin man.

2 What might Mr Crowther have thought was in the suitcase which Mr Harraby-Ribston threw out of the window?

  a Some old clothes.
  b Nothing at all.
  c A dead body.
  d Some stolen property.

3 While the suitcase was being thrown out of the window, Mr Crowther was

  a looking out of the window.
  b fast asleep.
  c writing a letter.
  d pretending to read a book.

4 What did Mr Harraby-Ribston feel about Mr Crowther's lack of reaction?

  a He was frightened.
  b He didn't care.
  c He was surprised.
  d He began to laugh.

Reading Comprehension

I

Complete the sentences in the following:

1 When Mr Crowther saw the man throw the suitcase out of the window he

  a tried to stop him.
  b said he would inform the police.
  c showed no interest.
  d became very angry.

2 The man said that he had thrown his suitcase out of the window because

  a he was in a bad temper.
  b he wanted to forget his past life.
  c he wanted to attract attention to himself.
  d his wife had left him.

3 Mr Harraby-Ribston said his way of supplying his friends with vegetables was

a not a well-known one.
b a good way of saving money.
c used by many people.
d forbidden by the railway.

II

Complete the following sentences in your own words:

1 The train was travelling at sixty miles an hour when . . .
2 Mr Crowther appeared not to notice what his companion had done, but actually . . .
3 It was probably the first time that Mr Crowther had ever seen . . .
4 Mr Crowther was not at all surprised when his companion told him . . .
5 Mr Crowther was very fond of his home because . . .
6 Throwing the suitcase out of the window was a primitive method, said Mr Harraby-Ribston, but . . .

III

Which of the following best expresses the opposite meaning of the word

1 prosperous. (107,3)

a unsuccessful.
b miserable.
c petulant.
d repressed.

2 loquacious. (107,15)

a devious.
b reserved.
c turbulent.
d pugnacious.

3 violent. (107,31)

a fragile.
b gentle.
c sensuous.
d incredulous.

114

4 trivial. (108,23)

 a clever.
 b impatient.
 c impersonal.
 d important.

5 reticence. (110,14)

 a ambiguity.
 b credulity.
 c frankness.
 d benevolence.

6 primitive. (111,8)

 a advanced.
 b sensible.
 c irrelevant.
 d plausible.

IV

After reading the whole story, answer the following questions:

1 What was the occupation of Mr Harraby-Ribston.
2 What was it that surprised Mr Crowther very much about the well-to-do gentleman?
3 What was Mr Crowther pretending to do while his companion threw out the suitcase?
4 How long had Mr Harraby-Ribston been married, did he say?
5 What did Mr Crowther say about his house?
6 What did Mr Crowther say had happened to his wife?
7 What did Mr Harraby-Ribston say was the truth about his own wife?

Discussion

1 How would you describe Mr Harraby-Ribston? Is he the kind of man you would like to have as a travelling companion?
2 What did you think of Mr Crowther's behaviour on the train? Did you think he was unusually calm and quiet in the circumstances? Perhaps he really did think it was a practical joke – or did he?
3 If you had been in the compartment, how would you have reacted?

4 Do you think there is much to choose between the two men, so far as character is concerned? Try to describe *(a)* their differences *(b)* their similarities.

5 What is your opinion of the title of this story? Do you agree that it is a good one, considering the final confessions of the two men?

Role-play

Divide up into pairs. Pretend you are in a railway compartment on a long journey. One of you wants to talk, the other doesn't want to be disturbed. Take it in turn to try and start a conversation.

Grammar Points

I Be going to + verb

Well, he wasn't going to jump, he wasn't going to pander to that sort of thing. (108,3)

Complete the following sentences, using the expression *be going to (intend to)*.

The thoughts of Mr Crowther on the train
1 It . . . be a nice peaceful journey.
2 Oh dear, what . . . that man . . . do?
3 I do believe he . . . throw his suitcase out of the window.
4 Oh well, I . . . not . . . take any notice.
5 Perhaps he . . . throw himself out of the window, too.
6 You never know what some people . . . do.
7 And I thought this compartment . . . be a quiet one.

II Third conditional with *have*

Now if you had thrown your suitcase out of the window, I should have been extremely curious to know why you did it. (109,5)

Complete the following sentences, using the correct form of the verb *have*:

1 If you . . . been on the train you . . . seen Mr Harraby-Ribston rise from his seat and throw his suitcase out of the window.
2 Mr Crowther . . . not . . . gone on reading if the suitcase . . . been his.

116

3 I know I . . . not . . . been able to keep quiet if I . . . been there.
4 If Mr Harraby-Ribston . . . not been so curious, he . . . not . . . spoken to Mr Crowther.
5 They . . . travelled in complete silence if the suitcase incident . . . not happened.

Words and Phrases

I

buzz around: move round and round. (107,23)
for all his appearance of apathy: in spite of the fact that he seemed to be uninterested. (107,27)
Highland Fling: a dance common in Scotland. (108,21)
I'm no chicken: I'm not young. (109,19)
in your line: suitable for you. (110,10)
Quite! Quite!: Of course! You are right! (110,29)

II

This story has been written in a rather literary style. Rewrite the first page in a colloquial style, choosing simple words instead of the more difficult ones.

The Invisible Japanese Gentlemen

Graham Greene

There were eight Japanese gentlemen having a fish dinner at Bentley's. They spoke to each other rarely in their incomprehensible tongue, but always with a courteous smile and often with a small bow. All but one of them wore glasses. Sometimes the pretty girl who sat in the window beyond gave them a passing glance, but her own problem seemed too serious for her to pay real attention to anyone in the world except herself and her companion.

She had thin blonde hair and her face was pretty and *petite* in a Regency way, oval like a miniature, though she had a harsh way of speaking – perhaps the accent of the school, Roedean or Cheltenham Ladies' College, which she had not long ago left. She wore a man's signet-ring on her engagement finger, and as I sat down at my table, with the Japanese gentlemen between us, she said, 'So you see we could marry next week.'

'Yes?'

Her companion appeared a little distraught. He refilled their glasses with Chablis and said, 'Of course, but Mother . . .' I missed some of the conversation then, because the eldest Japanese gentleman leant across the table, with a smile and a little bow, and uttered a whole paragraph like the mutter from an aviary, while everyone bent towards him and smiled and listened, and I couldn't help attending to him myself.

The girl's fiancé resembled her physically. I could see them as two miniatures hanging side by side on white wood panels. He should have been a young officer in Nelson's navy in the days when a certain weakness and sensitivity were no bar to promotion.

She said, 'They are giving me an advance of five hundred pounds, and they've sold the paperback rights already.' The hard commercial declaration came as a shock to me; it was a shock too that she was one of my own profession. She couldn't have been more than twenty. She deserved better of life.

He said, 'But my uncle . . .'

118

'You know you don't get on with him. This way we shall be quite independent.'

'*You* will be independent,' he said grudgingly.

'The wine-trade wouldn't really suit you, would it? I spoke to my publisher about you and there's a very good chance . . . if you began with some reading . . .'

'But I don't know a thing about books.'

'I would help you at the start.'

'My mother says that writing is a good crutch . . .'

'Five hundred pounds and half the paperback rights is a pretty solid crutch,' she said.

'This Chablis is good, isn't it?'

'I daresay.'

I began to change my opinion of him – he had not the Nelson touch. He was doomed to defeat. She came alongside and raked him fore and aft. 'Do you know what Mr Dwight said?'

'Who's Dwight?'

'Darling, you don't listen, do you? My publisher. He said he hadn't read a first novel in the last ten years which showed such powers of observation.'

'That's wonderful,' he said sadly, 'wonderful.'

'Only he wants me to change the title.'

'Yes?'

'He doesn't like *The Ever-Rolling Stream*. He wants to call it *The Chelsea Set*.'

'What did you say?'

'I agreed. I do think that with a first novel one should try to keep one's publisher happy. Especially when, really, he's going to pay for our marriage, isn't he?'

'I see what you mean.' Absent-mindedly he stirred his Chablis with a fork – perhaps before the engagement he had always bought champagne. The Japanese gentlemen had finished their fish and with very little English but with elaborate courtesy they were ordering from the middle-aged waitress a fresh fruit salad. The girl looked at them, and then she looked at me, but I think she saw only the future. I wanted very much to warn her against any future based on a first novel called *The Chelsea Set*. I was on the side of his mother. It was a humiliating thought, but I was probably about her mother's age.

I wanted to say to her, Are you certain your publisher is telling you the

truth? Publishers are human. They may sometimes exaggerate the virtues of the young and the pretty. Will *The Chelsea Set* be read in five years? Are you prepared for the years of effort, 'the long defeat of doing nothing well'? As the years pass writing will not become any easier, the daily
5   effort will grow harder to endure, those 'powers of observation' will become enfeebled; you will be judged, when you reach your forties, by performance and not by promise.

    'My next novel is going to be about St Tropez.'

    'I didn't know you'd ever been there.'

10   'I haven't. A fresh eye's terribly important. I thought we might settle down there for six months.'

    'There wouldn't be much left of the advance by that time.'

    'The advance is only an advance. I get fifteen per cent after five thousand copies and twenty per cent after ten. And of course another
15   advance will be due, darling, when the next book's finished. A bigger one if *The Chelsea Set* sells well.'

    'Suppose it doesn't.'

    'Mr Dwight says it will. He ought to know.'

    'My uncle would start me at twelve hundred.'

20   'But darling, how could you come then to St Tropez?'

    'Perhaps we'd do better to marry when you come back.'

    She said harshly, 'I mightn't come back if *The Chelsea Set* sells enough.'

    'Oh.'

    She looked at me and the party of Japanese gentlemen. She finished
25   her wine. She said, 'Is this a quarrel?'

    'No.'

    'I've got the title for the next book – *The Azure Blue*.'

    'I thought azure *was* blue.'

    She looked at him with disappointment. 'You don't really want to be
30   married to a novelist, do you?'

    'You aren't one yet.'

    'I was born one – Mr Dwight says. My powers of observation . . .'

    'Yes. You told me that, but, dear, couldn't you observe a bit nearer home? Here in London.'

35   'I've done that in *The Chelsea Set*. I don't want to repeat myself.'

    The bill had been lying beside them for some time now. He took out his wallet to pay, but she snatched the paper out of his reach. She said. 'This is my celebration.'

    'What of?'

'*The Chelsea Set,* of course. Darling, you're awfully decorative, but sometimes – well, you simply don't connect.'

'I'd rather . . . if you don't mind . . .'

'No, darling, this is on me. And Mr Dwight, of course.'

5   He submitted just as two of the Japanese gentlemen gave tongue simultaneously, then stopped abruptly and bowed to each other, as though they were blocked in a doorway.

    I had thought the two young people matching miniatures, but what a contrast in fact there was. The same type of prettiness could contain
10 weakness and strength. Her Regency counterpart, I suppose, would have borne a dozen children without the aid of anaesthetics, while he would have fallen an easy victim to the first dark eyes in Naples. Would there one day be a dozen books on her shelf? They have to be born without an anaesthetic too. I found myself hoping that *The Chelsea Set* would prove
15 to be a disaster and that eventually she would take up photographic modelling while he established himself solidly in the wine-trade in St James's. I didn't like to think of her as the Mrs Humphrey Ward of her generation – not that I would live so long. Old age saves us from the realization of a great many fears. I wondered to which publishing firm
20 Dwight belonged. I could imagine the blurb he would have already written about her abrasive powers of observation. There would be a photo, if he was wise, on the back of the jacket, for reviewers, as well as publishers, are human, and she didn't look like Mrs Humphrey Ward.

    I could hear them talking while they found their coats at the back of the
25 restaurant. He said, 'I wonder what all those Japanese are doing here?'

    'Japanese?' she said. 'What Japanese, darling? Sometimes you are so evasive I think you don't want to marry me at all.'

Questions

The Author

Graham Greene (1904–1991) was born in Hertfordshire and educated at Berkhamsted and Oxford. He was a novelist, dramatist and short story writer. His novels include *The Power and the Glory* (1940), *The Heart of the Matter* (1948), *The Honorary Consul* (1973) and *The Captain and the Enemy* (1988).

The Story

While the author is in a restaurant, he listens in to a conversation at another table between a pretty girl and her fiancé. The girl has just had her first novel accepted for publication and she has little interest in anything else.

Points to Consider

While reading the story, think about the following:

(a) the use of adjectives, unusual figures of speech, words or phrases revealing characters or expressing emotion.

(b) how a polite conflict is developed between two people who are normally very close to each other.

Listening Comprehension

True or False? (118,1–119,38)

1 All but one of the Japanese gentlemen were without glasses.
2 The girl in the story was wearing a diamond engagement ring.
3 The girl wanted to get married very soon.
4 The young man showed a lot of interest in becoming a writer.
5 The girl's publisher was named Dwight.

Reading Comprehension

I

Choose the correct answer in the following:

1 Instead of the word 'courteous' in the phrase 'a courteous smile' (118,3), the author could have used

   a obedient.
   b casual.
   c considerate.
   d reluctant.

2 The 'mutter from an aviary' (118,20), makes you think of

   a the sound of flying geese.
   b bees in an orchard.

   c the wind blowing through the trees.
   d the sound from a bird house.

3 The girl's companion appeared a little distraught (118,16) because he didn't like

   a sitting so close to the Japanese gentlemen.
   b the Chablis they were drinking.
   c other people looking at him.
   d the idea of getting married next week.

4 Why was it humiliating for the author? (119,37)

   a He couldn't tell the girl what he wanted.
   b He didn't like to think that he was as old as the girl's mother.
   c He didn't like the young man's mother.
   d He didn't want to be on the side of the young man.

II

Rewrite the following sentences from the story in your own words:

1 'You will be independent', he said grudgingly. (119,3)
2 I began to change my opinion of him – he had not the Nelson touch. (119,14)
3 He submitted just as two of the Japanese gentlemen gave tongue simultaneously. (121,5)
4 'Darling, you're awfully decorative, but sometimes – well, you simply don't connect.' (121,1)

III

After reading the whole story, answer these questions:

1 How many of the Japanese gentlemen wore glasses?
2 Where in the restaurant did the girl sit?
3 In what way did the girl's fiancé resemble her?
4 How much was the advance on the girl's first book?
5 How much did the girl's fiancé know about books?
6 Who was Mr Dwight?
7 What did the girl agree to in order to keep her publisher happy?
8 What did the Japanese gentlemen order from the middle-aged waitress?
9 What was the girl's next novel to be about?
10 When did her fiancé think they should get married?
11 What was to be the title of the girl's next book?
12 Why did she insist on paying for their meal at the restaurant?
13 How did her companion react to this idea?
14 What made the girl think that he didn't want to marry her?

Discussion

1 What did you think of the story? The characters? The comments by the author? What was the point of the story, do you think?
2 Give a description of the girl in the restaurant.
3 Describe her fiancé.
4 What kind of relationship do they have? Do you think they would be happy with each other in the future? Why/why not?
5 The author plays quite an important part in the story. Comment on his powers of observation and give examples. Could the Japanese gentlemen have been left out of the story? Why/why not?
6 What did you think of the title of the story?

Written Work

Imagine you are a detective following one of the Japanese gentlemen. Write a short description of the physical layout of the restaurant which you are to include in your report. Include as much detail as you can derive from the story and make up some details of your own if you wish.

Role-play

I

This story contains a great deal of dialogue. Why not try acting the conversation between the girl and her fiancé? Leave out the sections where the author interrupts, and add to the conversation where you feel it is necessary. Work in pairs so that everyone in the class has a chance to act.

II

First of all, find a printed menu, or make one up.

Work in threes. One of you can be a waiter or waitress, and the other two can order dinner from the menu – starter, main course and dessert. The following phrases may be useful:

Waiter Would you like a starter/anything to drink, Sir/Madam?
What would you like as your main course?
Do you want your steak well done, medium or rare?
Would you like a dessert/some coffee?
I hope you enjoyed your meal.

Customers May we see the menu/wine list, please.
I think I'd like . . . .
Waiter, may we have the bill?
Is the service charge included?
Thank you, that was very nice.

Grammar Points

I Tag questions

'The wine-trade wouldn't really suit you, would it?' (119,4)
'This Chablis is good, isn't it?' (119,12)
'Darling, you don't listen, do you?' (119,18)

Tag questions can be used when you want someone to agree with you. Put the correct tag questions in the following sentences.

1 Her publisher was very good, . . . ?
2 He wanted her to change the title, . . . ?
3 He isn't going to marry her, . . . ?

125

4 There are a lot of Japanese gentlemen here, . . . ?
5 You could hear them talking, . . . ?

II Direct and Indirect speech.

'Are you certain your publisher is telling you the truth?' he asked her.
=He asked her whether her publisher was telling her the truth.

Rewrite the following sentences in indirect speech, changing the verb form in each case.

1 'Will *The Chelsea Set* be read in five years?' he asked.
2 'Are you prepared for the years of effort?' he asked her.
3 'Writing will not become any easier,' he told her.
4 'You will be judged by performance, not by promise,' he told her.

III Polite disagreement

When you want to disagree with a suggestion in a polite way, you often use the expression 'I'd rather . . . , if you don't mind.'

A: Shall we go to Bournemouth on Sunday?
B: I'd rather go to Brighton, if you don't mind.

Divide up into pairs. One of you is **A** and the other **B**. **A** chooses a suggestion from the **A** list and **B** disagrees politely, giving a suitable reason from the **B** list. Add your own alternatives if you like.

A: have dinner at 5 o'clock today   **B:** go by bicycle
    go for a walk   have dinner at 6 o'clock
    put up at a hotel   have a read
    take the car   have a cup of tea
    order a pot of coffee   go camping

Words and Phrases

I

Roedean: famous public school for girls in England. (118,10)
Cheltenham Ladies' College: as above. (118,10)
engagement finger: third finger of left hand, on which engagement ring is worn. (118,12)
Chablis: French white Burgundy wine. (118,17)
Nelson: (1758–1805) great English naval commander. (118,24)

paperback rights: the right to produce the book with a soft cover. (118,27)
crutch: help on the side, not as one's main source of income. (119,11)
the Nelson touch: brave way of dealing with a situation. (119,14)
alongside: next to (about a ship). (119,15)
rake fore and aft: (about a ship) fire with guns at another ship from one end to the other. (119,15). Greene is still thinking about Nelson and saying that this young man, unlike Nelson, is allowing himself to be beaten in battle by the young lady, who is like an attacking ship.
Chelsea: part of London well known for artists and fashion. (119,25)
set: group of people. (119,25)
connect: think of things as being connected with one another. (121,2)
this is on me: I'm paying for this. (121,4)
give tongue: start speaking. (121,5)
photographic modelling: being photographed for advertisements. (121,15)
St James's: area of London around St James's Park, centre of the wine trade. (121,16)
Mrs Humphrey Ward: (1851–1920) conventional woman novelist. (121,17)

II

You will have noticed the author's powers of observation in this story. Collect examples of adjectives and adverbs which help to make you aware of this, e.g. a *fish* dinner, a *courteous* smile.

The Tractor

Peter Cowan

She watched him coming back from the gate, walking towards the slightly
ornate suburban style house she felt to be so incongruous set down on the
bare rise, behind it the sheds and yards and the thin belt of shade trees.
Yet he and his family were proud of it, grateful for its convenience and
5 modernity, and had so clearly not understood her first quizzical remarks
that she had never repeated them.

He stood on the edge of the veranda, and she saw in his face the anger
that seemed to deepen because he knew the feeling to be impotent. She
asked:

10 'What is it?'

'Mackay's two big tractors – that they were going to use for the scrub
clearing – they've been interfered with. Sand put into the oil. The one
they started up will cost a few hundred to repair.'

'But no one would do that,' she said, as if already it were settled, her
15 temporizing without point.

'We know who did it.'

'Surely he didn't come right up to the sheds – so close as that to the
house . . .'

'No. They left the tractors down in the bottom paddock. Where they
20 were going to begin clearing.'

'And now – they can't?'

'Now they can't. Not till the tractor's repaired.'

She looked towards the distant line of the low scrub that was deepening
in colour as the evening came. She said:

25 'That is what he wanted.'

'What he wants is to make as much trouble as he can. We haven't done
anything to him.'

'You were going to clear the land along the bottom paddock at the back
of Mackay's. Where he lives.'

30 'Where he lives?'

'You told me he lived in the bush there.'

128

'He lives anywhere. And he takes the ball-floats off the taps of the sheep tanks and the water runs to waste, and he breaks the fence when he feels like it, and leaves the gates open . . .'

'You think he does this deliberately?'

'How else?'

'Oh,' she said, 'yet it's all so ruthless.'

'You mean what he does?'

'No. You only ever think of what he does.'

'Well, I'll admit he's given us a few things to think about.'

'Clearing with those tractors and the chain,' she said. 'Everything in their path goes – kangaroos, all the small things that live in the scrub – all the trees . . .'

He looked at her as if her words held some relevance that must come to him. He said:

'We clear the land. Yes.'

'You clear it,' she said. 'It seems to be what is happening everywhere today.'

'I don't know what you mean, Ann.'

She got up from the chair by the steps. 'Perhaps he feels something should be left.'

'Look,' he said, 'maybe you teach too much nature study at school. Or you read all this stuff about how we shouldn't shoot the bloody 'roos – so that when some crazy swine wrecks our property you think he's some sort of a . . .'

'Some sort of what?'

'I don't know,' he said, aware she mocked him. 'Better than us.'

'No. Perhaps just different.'

'Different all right.'

'What are you going to do?'

'Get the police,' he said. 'They don't take much notice most of the time, but they will of this.' He looked at her as if he would provoke the calm he felt to be assumed. 'We'll burn him out if we can't get him any other way.'

She looked up quickly and for a moment he was afraid.

'You wouldn't do that.'

'He's gone too far this time,' he said stubbornly.

The long thin streamers of cloud above the darkening line of scrub were becoming deep and hard in colour, scarlet against the dying light. He watched her face that seemed now calm, remote, as if their words were erased. She was small, slight, somehow always neat, contained. Her dark hair was drawn straight back, her brows clearly marked, lifting slightly so that they seemed to give sometimes humour to her serious expression, her firm mouth.

'I'd better go, Ken.'

5 'The family expect you for tea.'

'It's Sunday night. I've to work in the morning. I have some things to prepare.'

'Look,' he said. 'If it's this business . . .'

'No. I'm just tired. And I've assignments to mark.'

10 'All right.'

As they drove she watched the long shadows that spread across the road and over the paddocks from the few shade trees, the light now possessing a clarity denied through the heat of the day. She would have liked to make some gesture to break the tension between them, to explain

15 to him why she had been unwilling to stay and listen to the inevitable talk of what had happened. But to tell him that at such times she became afraid, as if she could never become one of them, certain that the disagreements which were now easily enough brought to a truce must in the end defeat them, would not lessen their dissension. He said suddenly:

20 'You're worried about it, aren't you.'

She knew he referred to themselves, as though he had been aware of her own thoughts.

'Yes,' she said. 'Sometimes.'

'It could be all right, Ann. You'd come to like it here.'

25 'In so many ways I do.'

'It's nothing like it used to be. This light land has come good now. We've done well. We've got everything – you wouldn't be without anything you'd have in the city.'

'I know that, Ken.'

30 'But you're not sure of it.'

She thought he perhaps did this deliberately, seeking to provoke an issue on material grounds, as if these at least were demonstrable of some conclusion, that he was lost, unwilling, in the face of their real uncertainty. He was more perceptive, she knew, than he cared to reveal,

35 but he had a stubbornness she felt it was perhaps impossible to defeat. Before it, she relented a little.

'Not sure of some things. You must give me time. After all, I – hadn't thought to live here. It's different for you.'

The few high trees stood out darkly above the low thick scrub, and beyond she could see the roofs of the town. He said:

'This other business will probably be over next week, anyhow.'

She supposed he deliberately minimized this which perhaps he did not understand, preferring evasion, the pretence that when it was settled it would not matter. As to him it might not. But he was so clearly afraid that she would escape. She reached out quickly and touched his hand.

He stopped the car before the house near the end of the main street, where she boarded. Further down, near the club, she could see the cars parked, and people moving without haste along the pavements.

There was no wind, and in the darkness the street was hot, as if the endless heat of summer was never to be dissipated. As he closed the door of the car he said:

'I have to go out to the paddock on the way back. It won't take long.'

She made no comment and he said, as if to prevent her censure:

'I've got to take some stuff from the store out there.'

'They haven't found him?'

'No. The police think he's moved out. But we know he hasn't. He makes fools of them in the bush. They've been looking since Sunday, but they've given it up now. Anyhow, you could walk right past him at three feet. And there are no tracks.'

'To be able to dodge them like that he must know all this country very well.'

'I suppose he does.'

'Almost – more than that. He must understand it.'

'He doesn't seem to do anything else all day.'

She smiled. 'Well, do you?'

'I'm not sure what you mean by that. You mean we don't understand it?'

'Perhaps in a different way. You're making it something you can understand.'

'Here we go again.' He banged his hand against the steering wheel. 'We never take a trick. Why don't you go and live with this character.'

She laughed suddenly. 'I'm sorry, Ken. But how long has he been here? That's a harmless enough question!'

'He's been around here something like ten years. I remember when I was at school. He's mad.'

She said: 'All those who oppose us are mad.'

'Well, we're going to get him out this time. We're taking shifts down at the tractors, and we've got a watch on a camp of his we found.'

'A camp?'

'Made out of boughs.' His voice was grudging. 'Pretty well made. You could live in it. We flushed him out, because he left some food, and a radio.'

5   'That's not in keeping – a radio . . .'

'It doesn't work. May never have been any good. It might be only that the batteries are flat. We'll find out. But he could have camps like that all through the bush. We'll be lucky if he comes back to this one.'

They turned off through a fence gate, and down along a track that
10   followed a side fence. He switched off the car lights and drove slowly.

'He'll hear the car,' he said. 'Still, the lights are a give-away.'

Suddenly they were close to the dark thick scrub, and then she saw the forms of the tractors, gaunt, high, like grotesque patches of shadow. Two men moved up to the car. One of them began to say something, then saw
15   her, and paused. He said:

'He came back, Ken. Got the food. We never saw him.'

They carried rifles, and suddenly she began to laugh. They looked at her with a surprise that had not yet become hostility.

'It – it just seems funny,' she said weakly.

20   'It's not funny,' Ken said. She was aware of their anger.

'We'll get him,' the man she recognized as Don Mackay said. 'We'll get him this time.'

She was reminded of the boys at school in the playground at the lunch period, confronted by some argument which physical force could not
25   immediately solve. Even their voices sound alike, she thought. Perhaps it is not so serious. But when they had taken the box Ken handed out to them, and as they stepped back from the car she saw again the guns they carried, and the parallel frightened her.

'How long will they be repairing the tractor?' she asked.

30   'End of the week.' His voice was brusque. She knew she had belittled him before his friends. She moved closer to him as he drove, and he looked briefly at her small serious face shadowed in the half-light of the car.

'We'll go through there next week. I wish he'd get between the tractors
35   when they're dragging the chain, that's all.'

'Is he armed?'

'Yes,' he said. 'He is. He's lived off the land for years. And by taking food. He might be dangerous now.'

She said slowly: 'I wonder what made him begin to live like that?'

'No one will know that.'

'You'll have to take care.'

'There'll be a few of us there to watch for him.'

'Actually, he hasn't ever threatened anyone, has he?'

'No. But he's never damaged anything big like this. And the police have never bothered about him before, either. You can see why. He's made fools of them.'

'And of you.'

'All right. And of us.'

'Oh, Ken,' she said. 'I'm sorry. It's – it's just that I wish somehow you could just let him be.'

'And have him do what he likes?'

'Well, he's not done anything much.'

'Only wrecked a tractor.'

'He would hate the tractors,' she said, as if she no longer spoke to him but was trying to work something out to her own satisfaction.

'Well, it's a reason why we can't leave him there.'

'I suppose you *have* to clear that land?'

'Of course. We clear some land every year. It's a tax deduction. And we need it the way taxation is.'

'So there can't be anybody who wants things to stay the way they are for a while?'

He looked at her strangely. 'Stay the way they are?'

If it was not what she meant she could not perhaps find words that were any more adequate. It was not a simple thing of statement, of definition, this which she felt. She saw with a sudden desolating clarity the grey sprawl of suburbs crossed by the black lines of roads, the clusters of city buildings, the endless tawdry, over-decorated little houses like the one he and his family had placed on the long low rise of land from which almost all else had been erased. As though, she thought painfully, he hated this land she had herself, incongruously enough, come to feel for in the brief time she had been close to it. And it was perhaps worse that he did not see what he was doing, himself a part of some force beyond him. Duped by pride. It was as if she had made some discovery she could not communicate to him, and that set them apart. She said desperately:

'Do we have to change everything? Wipe out everything so that everlastingly we can grow things, make things, get tax deductions? You don't even leave a few acres of timber, somewhere for animals and birds . . .'

'Animals and birds,' he said. 'You can't stop progress.'

'The unanswerable answer.' Before them the shade trees showed briefly along the road as it turned near the farm. 'So we must all conform.'

He slowed the car for the house gate, and in the headlights she saw the
5 façade of the house as if they had turned into a suburban street. As he stopped the motor the silence held them. For a moment they did not move, then he drew her against him, his arm lightly about her shoulders, the gesture token of a security they might both have willed, denying the words with which they had held themselves separate.

10 'Maybe,' he said slowly, 'it's because you're so crazy I have to have you. You – you're different . . .'

'I'm sorry, Ken. Because I'm afraid I do love you – I suppose I have to have you, too.'

'And you'd rather you didn't.'

15 'Perhaps I would rather I didn't.'

'It's a mess, isn't it.'

'It might sort out,' she said, and laughed with him. At the house the front door opened briefly, the light shining across the entrance porch as someone looked out at the car.

20 In the weekend she had arranged to stay at the farm, and she expected him to call for her soon after breakfast. She put her small case on the veranda, but as he did not come she went back inside. Idly, rather irritated at his lateness, she took out her paints and began to work on the flower illustrations she was making. She had begun to paint the native flowers,
25 their grotesque seeds and leaves, to use for her teaching, but the work had begun to absorb her, and she spent whatever time she could searching for new examples. Many, at first, she could not identify. Now, though she told no one, she had begun to hope the paintings might be publishable if she could complete series of different areas.

30 It was mid-morning when she heard him outside. In the car as they drove he said:

'Some of the fences were broken, out by Hadley's boundary. We've been too busy this week to look down there, and the sheep had gone through into the scrub. We got most of them back.'

35 'You lost some?'

'Some.'

'I'm sorry,' she said, as though somehow it were her fault.

'He knows we're going to clear that land, and he's out to do as much damage as he can first.'

She had no wish to draw him, as if she deliberately sought their disagreement, but it seemed she must form the words, place them before him, his evasion too easy.

'You're sure about it, Ken, aren't you. That he's just getting his own back? That it's as simple as that.'

'It's obvious. He's done pretty well so far.'

'And that's the only side there is to it?'

'What else could there be? He can't expect to stop us.'

'He might know that.'

'Well – that proves it.'

'No – perhaps we've all got to make a gesture of some sort. For the things we believe in.'

He shook his head. 'You put it your way if you like. But what I believe in is using that land.'

'Yes, Ken.'

'We can't all be dreamers.' And then as though he refused to be further drawn he laughed. 'It's funny the way I've got caught up with one. Perhaps it will sort out, as you said. You do the dreaming. I'll do the work.'

She ran her hands lightly over her arms, smiling at him. 'You think we might convert one another?'

'It's a risk we'll have to take.'

'Yes. I suppose we're young enough.'

'I'll be out a bit this weekend, Ann. We've got to stop this somehow. While we've a few sheep left.'

He went out late in the afternoon, and she helped his mother in the kitchen. The older woman had a quietness, and a kind of insight that she found attractive, and they had always got on well together, though sometimes Ann was irritated by her acceptance of the men's decisions and views, as if this was something she no longer questioned, or perhaps, Ann thought, she had never questioned.

When Ken came back she heard him talking to his father on the veranda, and then the older man's voice raised in disagreement, though she could distinguish only a few of the words. She went out through the kitchen door and the men stopped talking. As she came towards them Ken said:

'We've found one of his camps. Ted and Don found it, but this time they turned off and kept away. They didn't go near enough for him to realize they'd seen it. We made that mistake last time.'

'Where is this?'

'It's new. So he may still be there. It's down in the paddock off the side road to Mackay's. Straight in from the dam. About half a mile north in the scrub.'

5   'There.'

'Yes. By the new land. Where we were going to build.' He looked at her as if she might have contradicted him. 'When we were married.'

'What will you do?'

His father said: 'I told them to get the police.'

10   'He walked away from the police last time.' For a moment his eyes met the girl's. 'And us. All right. We were no better. And the reporters came up from town. Photographers all over the place. A seven-day wonder for the suburbanites.'

'It's not something that happens every day,' she said. 'Naturally, it was
15 news.'

'They'll make it news again, if we let them. But this time it will be different. We don't do anything until tomorrow night. That way he won't be suspicious if he sees our tracks near the camp. Then Sunday night we'll make a line north of the camp, and if the wind's right we'll burn back
20 towards the firebreak along the paddock. He'll have to break out through the paddock. We'll have a chance that way.'

'I think it's too big a risk,' his father said. 'You'll burn the whole of that country. You can't do it.'

'We were going to clear it, anyway.'

25   'You can't start a fire like that.'

'If we try to close in on the camp he'll hear us.'

'You could still get him. There's enough of you.'

'He'd go between us in the bush. No matter how close we were. You know that. No one's been able to get a sight of him in the bush. The police
30 had trackers there last week. They found plenty of tracks. But he kept as far ahead or behind them as he liked. No,' he added, 'he's made fools of us long enough. I think we've got a chance now.'

He turned towards the girl, and she stood beside him, not moving. His words seemed to her to hold a kind of defiance as if he did not himself
35 believe in them, and she thought that it was not simply that he doubted their ability to carry out the plan, but that he did not really believe in the idea of the fire himself. That if she or his father did not further pursue it he might be glad to drop it. But she could not be certain, and before she could speak, as if he intended to prevent her words, he said:

136

'Let's forget this now, Ann. We'll go over to Harris's after tea. They've got a bit of a show on there for May's birthday.'

Almost all those she had come to know seemed to have found their way to the party. And all of them discussed the hermit, as they called him. She
5   realized it was general knowledge that he was expected to be caught soon. She listened to the undercurrent of derision that the police with all their resources had been mocked by this man it seemed none of them had seen, as if in this they were on his side. Some of the older people she spoke to claimed to have caught glimpses of him when, some years earlier, he had
10 taken food quite freely for a time from the farm houses. Some claimed to know his name. But it seemed to her, as she mixed with them and listened to them that none of them really cared. She felt they simply accepted the idea that he must be denied, driven from cover and killed if necessary, as they might have accepted the killing of a dingo or a fox, a creature for
15 them without motive or reason. When she tried to turn their words, to question them, they looked at her with a kind of surprise, or the beginning of suspicion, perhaps in doubt of her as a teacher of their children. And she saw that quite quickly they exhausted the topic, turning to the enjoyment of the evening, as if already the whole thing was disposed of.
20 In the end she thought it was their lack of involvement, their bland rejection of responsibility, that irritated her to the point of anger, so that she was forced to hold herself from rudeness.

It was late when they returned, and in her room, after she had changed, she stood for a time by the window in the darkness. There was a small
25 moon that seemed scarcely to break the dark ground shadow, and beyond the paddocks she could not see where the scrub began. Her sense of anger had given place to dejection and a kind of fear. She tried to imagine the man who in the darkness slept in what they had described as his camp, something she could picture only as a kind of child's cubby house in the
30 thick scrub. But she could form no picture of him as a physical being, only that it seemed to her he must possess imagination and sensibility beyond that of his pursuers; that he must be someone not difficult to talk to, someone who would understand her own feeling about these things for which he was persecuted. And who might even, she thought, be glad to
35 know, however briefly, that they were shared. She was aware of a sense of disloyalty, but the image persisted, and it was suddenly monstrous that the darkness of the scrub should be swept by the glare of fire, as she would

see it from the window where she stood now, the man stumbling from it in some unimaginable indignity. And though she had doubted the men's intention to carry out their plan, it seemed now in the darkness only too probable that in anger they might do what she, and perhaps they, feared.
5 And it was impossible. Her hands felt the cold of the sill, she was aware of the faint wind that blew in through the window, cool upon her skin, and she could hear it in the boughs of the few shade trees behind the house.

On Sunday, in the afternoon, Ken left to make arrangements with the other men. His parents were resting, but she knew they would not
10 question her going out; they were used to her wandering about the farm, looking for the plants she wished to paint. She went down through the yard gate, across the paddock towards the track that led out to the belt of scrub and timber. It seemed, in the heat, further than she had expected.
She walked along the side fence, where the brush began, feeling that it
15 would hide her if any of the men were watching. If she met them she would say she had come to look for Ken. She could see the dam ahead, the smooth red banks rising steeply, to one side a few thin trees, motionless in the heat.
At the dam she paused. The side track to Mackay's had turned some
20 distance back to the left. In front of her, facing north, the scrub was thick, untouched, she was suddenly reluctant to go beyond the fence on the far side of the dam.
She pushed the wires down and stepped through. She began to pick her way through the scrub, choosing the small, almost imperceptible pockets
25 where the bushes were thinner. It was only after a time, when she could no longer see the dam or the trees beside it, that she realized her method of walking had led her away from a straight line. She had no clear idea how far she had come. She went on until she was certain she had covered half a mile, but as she stopped it was suddenly clear she could have deviated in
30 any direction.
The bushes grew upward on their thin sparse stems to a rounded umbrella-like top, the leaves tough, elongated and spindly. They stretched away like endless replicas, rising head high, become too thick for her to go further. As she looked about, it seemed improbable she had
35 come so far. In the heat the scrub was silent. Along the reddish ground, over the thin stalks, the ants moved, in places she had walked round their mud-coloured mounds. She looked down at the ground, at the hard brittle twigs and fallen leaves, some of them already cemented by the ants. In a

kind of fear she began to walk.

A short distance to the right a thin patch of trees lifted above the bushes, and though she thought it was the wrong direction she began to push her way towards it. The trees were like some sharp variation in the
5 endless grey pattern of the brush that rose about her.

Beneath them the bark and leaves were thick upon the ground. She stood in the patch of shade, and she tried to reason that she could not have come far, that she could find her way back if she were careful. And in the silence she thought again, as she had the night before, of the man she had
10 come to warn. It had seemed that if she could explain to him, he must understand, and that perhaps he would go. She had relied on there being understanding between them, that at least in these things they must feel alike. So that it had seemed her words would have effect. Now, in the heat and the silence, it was a dream, holding in this place no reality. She could
15 never have thought to do it. And it was here he had spent ten years. It was like nothing she could encompass. She felt a sharp, childish misery, as if she might have allowed herself tears.

It occurred to her that if she could climb one of the trees she might gain an idea of direction. But the trunks were slippery, without foothold, and
20 at the second attempt she fell, twisting her leg. She leaned against the trunk, afraid of the pain, trying to deny it as if she would will herself to be without injury which might imprison her.

She was not aware of any movement or sound, but she looked up, and turned slightly, still holding to the smooth trunk. He was standing just at
25 the edge of the clump of trees. He might have been there all the time. Or been attracted by the noise she had made. She said weakly:

'I – didn't see you . . .'

His face held no expression she could read. His hair was grey and short – and she was vaguely surprised as if she had imagined something
30 different – but cut crudely, and streaked across his head by sweat. He was very thin as if all the redundant flesh had long ago been burned from him, his arms stick-like, knotted and black. His hands held a rifle, and she knew a sudden fear that he would kill her, that somehow she must place words between them before he took her simply as one of his persecutors.
35 She said quickly:

'I came to warn you – they have found your camp – tonight they mean to drive you out towards the paddocks . . .'

But they were not the words she had planned. His eyes gave her no sign. They were very dark, sharp somehow, and she knew they were like the eyes of an animal or a bird, watchful, with their own recognition and knowledge which was not hers. The stubble of beard across his face was whitish, his skin dark from the sun.

'I – if only you would go from here,' she said. 'They only want you to go
5   – they don't understand . . .'

The words were dead in the heat and the silence. She saw the flies that crawled across his face.

'I wanted to help you,' she said, and she despised herself in her terror. Only his hands seemed to move faintly about the rifle. His stillness was
10   insupportable. Abruptly she began to sob, the sound loud, gulping, ridiculous, her hands lifting to her face.

He seemed to step backwards. His movement was somehow liquid, unhuman, and then she thought of the natives she had once seen in the north, not the town natives whose movements had grown like her own.
15   But with a strange inevitability he moved like an animal or the vibration of the thin sparse trees before the wind. She did not see him go. She looked at the boles of the trees where he had stood, and she could hear her own sobbing.

Sometime in the afternoon she heard the sound of shots, flat, unreal, soon
20   lost in the silence. But she walked towards where the sound had seemed to be, and after a time, without warning she came into the track that ran towards Mackay's place. She had gone only a short distance when she heard the voices, and called out. The men came through the scrub and she saw them on the track. She began to run towards them, but checked
25   herself. Further down she saw a Land-Rover and one of the police. Ken said:

'We missed you – we've been searching – it was only that Ted saw where you'd walked down the fence . . .'

'The shots – I heard them . . .'
30   'We were looking for you. We didn't see him. He tried to get past us, then shot at Don – we had to shoot.'

She did not speak and he added: 'We had to do it, Ann. We sent for the police. But where were you – how did you get out here . . .'

There was nothing she could tell him. She said:
35   'I was looking for you, I think.'

The Land-Rover had drawn up beside them, and the driver opened the door for her. They moved back down the dry rutted track where the thin shade had begun to stretch in from the broken scrub.

Questions

The Author

Peter Cowan was born in 1914 in Perth, Western Australia. He has worked as a clerk, a farm worker, served in the Royal Australian Air Force and lectured in English at the University of Western Australia. He has published both short stories and novels.

The Story

The Tractor is set in Australia. The two main characters, Ann, a town-girl, and Ken, a sheep farmer, are soon to be married. However, they have basic differences of attitude towards the land and its use, which affects their relationship. These differences are also emphasized by their opposing views on how the hermit in the story should be regarded.

Points to Consider

While reading the story, think about the following:

(*a*) the detailed descriptions of the countryside.
(*b*) whether you agree with Ann's or Ken's attitude on how the land should be used.

Listening Comprehension

True or false? (138,8–140,38)

1 When Ann got to the dam, she suddenly became eager to go on.
2 She soon realized that she did not know in what direction she had walked.
3 She tried to climb one of the trees, but didn't succeed until the third attempt.
4 The man she met had long hair streaked with sweat.
5 He was carrying a gun.
6 The man gave himself up, but they shot him.

Reading Comprehension

I

After reading 128,1–137,2 answer the following questions:

1 What were the two tractors to be used for?
2 What had been put into the oil?
3 When could they begin clearing the scrub?
4 What happened when the ball-float was taken off the taps of the sheep tanks?
5 What did Ken say he would do about the man who was wrecking their property?
6 What was it in Ken which Ann felt was impossible to defeat?
7 As they drove along, what could Ann see beyond the scrub and the trees?
8 Besides a radio, what else did they find at the camp?
9 What benefit did Ken get from clearing the land?
10 What did Ken say couldn't be stopped?
11 Why was Ken's father afraid of starting a fire?
12 Who did all the people at the party discuss?

II

Choose the correct answer in the following:

1 Which of the words below means nearly the same as *reluctant?* (138,21)

    a afraid.
    b disinclined.
    c decided.
    d prepared.

2 Which of the words below means nearly the same as *improbable?* (138,34)

    a inescapable.
    b arguable.
    c unlikely.
    d impossible.

3 Which of the words below means the same as *redundant?* (139,31)

    a surrounding.
    b superfluous.
    c superficial.
    d supreme.

III

Choose the words from the list below which fit into the following sentences:

imperceptible, twig, ridiculous, paddock, sobbing, slippery, replica, sparse, misery, despise

1 He stood at the top of the . . . slope and looked down at the frozen sea.
2 The girl walked across the . . . where the horses were standing, and waited a while.
3 The child lay awake . . . .
4 After a short distance through the forest, she began to realize it was . . . to think that she could find her way alone.

IV

Rewrite the sentences below in your own words:

1 It was only after a time, when she could no longer see the dam or the trees beside it, that she realized her method of walking had led her away from a straight line.
2 She felt a sharp, childish misery, as if she might have allowed herself tears.
3 His face held no expression she could read.
4 His hands held a rifle, and she knew a sudden fear that he would kill her, that somehow she must place words between them before he took her simply as one of his persecutors.

Discussion

1 Describe Ann. What do we get to know about her? Her interests? Her attitude to people? Her attitude to nature, e.g. her opposition to Ken's scrub-clearing programme? Is she too sentimental about the countryside, do you think?
2 Ken. What is he like (*a*) as a farmer? (*b*) in his relationship with Ann? Do you see his attitude to his farming as progressive, or do you find him ruthless?
3 Comment on this quotation (134,10):
'Maybe,' he said slowly, 'it's because you're so crazy I have to have you. You – you're different . . . .'
'I'm sorry, Ken. Because I'm afraid I do love you – I suppose I have to have you, too.'
'And you'd rather you didn't.'
'Perhaps I would rather I didn't.'

What does it tell us about Ann's relationship with Ken? How do you think this will turn out?

4 What do you think of Ann's whole attitude to the hermit? Describe their meeting in your own words.

5 The 'tractor' in the title seems to be a kind of symbol. Of what?

General Discussion

What is happening to our environment?

'We clear the land. Yes.'
'You clear it,' she said. 'It seems to be what is happening everywhere today.' (129,15)

Nature is being polluted and our environment destroyed by modern machinery, waste products, smoke and fumes, etc. What, if anything, can be done to stop this? On an international level, on a national level and on a local level? Can an individual person help in any way?

Grammar Points

I Active to Passive

'The tractors have been interfered with,' (128,12)
= Someone has interfered with the tractors.

Put the following sentences into the passive:

1 The family expect you to tea.
2 The men cleared the land.
3 They teach too much nature study at school.
4 He broke the fences and left the gates open.
5 Ken had parked his car farther down the street.
6 The parallel frightened her.

II Some and any

'Well, he's not done anything much.' (133,13)
'Perhaps he feels something should be left.' (129,19)

Fill in the gaps below using *some* or *any*.

Ann had already had . . . doubts about whether she should marry Ken, but she had not been able to say . . . thing to him about it. Now that . . . of the tractors had been damaged, . . . of the tension between them had come out into the open. Ann felt that the man had hardly done . . . real damage and asked Ken why it wasn't possible to leave . . . things as they were, leave . . . where for the animals and birds. Wasn't there . . . place where nature could be left alone? . . . time later, Ann met the man. She tried to show him by . . . gesture that she hadn't . . . thing against him, that she only wanted to help him, to do . . . thing for him.

Words and Phrases

I

'roos: kangaroos. (129,22)
swine: vulgar word for 'a man'. (129,23)
flush out: drive out, cause to move. (132,3)
be in keeping: be in harmony with what one expects. (132,5)
a give-away: something that made their presence obvious. (132,11)
tax deduction: way of paying less tax. (133,19)
got caught up with: became associated with. (135,18)
a seven day wonder: normally a nine days' wonder; something which arouses interest for only a short time. (136,12)
suburbanites: people who live in the suburbs of the city. (136,13)
dingo: wild Australian dog. (137,14)
cubby house: small house built out of branches, etc., by child. (137,29)
Land-Rover: heavy car used for driving over rough ground. (140,25)

II

There are some almost photographic descriptions of landscape in the story, e.g. in the first paragraph. Pick out two or three other vivid descriptions and try to analyse how the author has written them. Are they particularly vivid because of the nouns, the adjectives or the verbs?

Parson's Pleasure

Roald Dahl

Mr Boggis was driving the car slowly, leaning back comfortably in the seat with one elbow resting on the sill of the open window. How beautiful the countryside, he thought; how pleasant to see a sign or two of summer once again. The primroses especially. And the hawthorn. The hawthorn
5   was exploding white and pink and red along the hedges and the primroses were growing underneath in little clumps, and it was beautiful.

He took one hand off the wheel and lit himself a cigarette. The best thing now, he told himself, would be to make for the top of Brill Hill. He could see it about half a mile ahead. And that must be the village of Brill,
10   that cluster of cottages among the trees right on the very summit. Excellent. Not many of his Sunday sections had a nice elevation like that to work from.

He drove up the hill and stopped the car just short of the summit on the outskirts of the village. Then he got out and looked around. Down below,
15   the countryside was spread out before him like a huge green carpet. He could see for miles. It was perfect. He took a pad and pencil from his pocket, leaned against the back of the car, and allowed his practised eye to travel slowly over the landscape.

He could see one medium farmhouse over on the right, back in the
20   fields, with a track leading to it from the road. There was another larger one beyond it. There was a house surrounded by tall elms that looked as though it might be a Queen Anne, and there were two likely farms away over on the left. Five places in all. That was about the lot in this direction.

Mr Boggis drew a rough sketch on his pad showing the position of each
25   so that he'd be able to find them easily when he was down below, then he got back into the car and drove up through the village to the other side of the hill. From there he spotted six more possibles – five farms and one big white Georgian house. He studied the Georgian house through his binoculars. It had a clean prosperous look, and the garden was well
30   ordered. That was a pity. He ruled it out immediately. There was no point in calling on the prosperous.

In this square then, in this section, there were ten possibilities in all. Ten was a nice number, Mr Boggis told himself. Just the right amount for a leisurely afternoon's work. What time was it now? Twelve o'clock. He would have liked a pint of beer in the pub before he started, but on
5 Sundays they didn't open until one. Very well, he would have it later. He glanced at the notes on his pad. He decided to take the Queen Anne first, the house with the elms. It had looked nicely dilapidated through the binoculars. The people there could probably do with some money. He was always lucky with Queen Annes, anyway. Mr Boggis climbed back
10 into the car, released the handbrake, and began cruising slowly down the hill without the engine.

Apart from the fact that he was at this moment disguised in the uniform of a clergyman, there was nothing very sinister about Mr Cyril Boggis. By trade he was a dealer in antique furniture, with his own shop and
15 showroom in the King's Road, Chelsea. His premises were not large, and generally he didn't do a great deal of business, but because he always bought cheap, very very cheap, and sold very very dear, he managed to make quite a tidy little income every year. He was a talented salesman, and when buying or selling a piece he could slide smoothly into whichever
20 mood suited the client best. He could become grave and charming for the aged, obsequious for the rich, sober for the godly, masterful for the weak, mischievous for the widow, arch and saucy for the spinster. He was well aware of his gift, using it shamelessly on every possible occasion; and often, at the end of an unusually good performance, it was as much as he
25 could do to prevent himself from turning aside and taking a bow or two as the thundering applause of the audience went rolling through the theatre.

In spite of this rather clownish quality of his, Mr Boggis was not a fool. In fact, it was said of him by some that he probably knew as much about French, English and Italian furniture as anyone else in London. He also
30 had surprisingly good taste, and he was quick to recognize and reject an ungraceful design, however genuine the article might be. His real love, naturally, was for the work of the great eighteenth-century English designers, Ince, Mayhew, Chippendale, Robert Adam, Manwaring, Inigo Jones, Hepplewhite, Kent, Johnson, George Smith, Lock, Sheraton, and
35 the rest of them, but even with these he occasionally drew the line. He refused, for example, to allow a single piece from Chippendale's Chinese or Gothic period to come into his showroom, and the same was true of some of the heavier Italian designs of Robert Adam.

During the past few years, Mr Boggis had achieved considerable fame

among his friends in the trade by his ability to produce unusual and often quite rare items with astonishing regularity. Apparently the man had a source of supply that was almost inexhaustible, a sort of private warehouse, and it seemed that all he had to do was to drive out to it once a
5   week and help himself. Whenever they asked him where he got the stuff he would smile knowingly and wink and murmur something about a little secret.

    The idea behind Mr Boggis's little secret was a simple one, and it had come to him as a result of something that had happened on a certain
10 Sunday afternoon nearly nine years before, while he was driving in the country.

    He had gone out in the morning to visit his old mother, who lived in Sevenoaks, and on the way back the fanbelt on his car had broken, causing the engine to overheat and the water to boil away. He had got out
15 of the car and walked to the nearest house, a smallish farm building about fifty yards off the road, and had asked the woman who answered the door if he could please have a jug of water.

    While he was waiting for her to fetch it, he happened to glance in through the door to the living-room, and there, not five yards from where
20 he was standing, he spotted something that made him so excited the sweat began to come out all over the top of his head. It was a large oak armchair of a type that he had only seen once before in his life. Each arm, as well as the panel at the back, was supported by a row of eight beautifully turned spindles. The back panel itself was decorated by an inlay of the most
25 delicate floral design, and the head of a duck was carved to lie along half the length of either arm. Good God, he thought. This thing is late fifteenth century!

    He poked his head in further through the door, and there, by heavens, was another of them on the other side of the fire-place!
30   He couldn't be sure, but two chairs like that must be worth at least a thousand pounds up in London. And oh, what beauties they were!

    When the woman returned, Mr Boggis introduced himself and straight away asked if she would like to sell her chairs.

    Dear me, she said. But why on earth should she want to sell her
35 chairs?

    No reason at all, except that he might be willing to give her a pretty nice price.

    And how much would he give? They were definitely not for sale, but just out of curiousity, just for fun, you known, how much would he give?

Thirty-five pounds.

How much?

Thirty-five pounds.

Dear me, thirty-five pounds. Well, well, that was very interesting.
5   She'd always thought they were valuable. They were very old. They were
very comfortable too. She couldn't possibly do without them, not
possibly. No, they were not for sale but thank you very much all the
same.

They weren't really so very old, Mr Boggis told her, and they wouldn't
10 be at all easy to sell, but it just happened that he had a client who rather
liked that sort of thing. Maybe he could go up another two pounds – call it
thirty-seven. How about that?

They bargained for half an hour, and of course in the end Mr Boggis got
the chairs and agreed to pay her something less than a twentieth of their
15 value.

That evening, driving back to London in his old station-wagon with the
two fabulous chairs tucked away snugly in the back, Mr Boggis had
suddenly been struck by what seemed to him to be a most remarkable
idea.

20 Look here, he said. If there is good stuff in one farmhouse, then why
not in others? Why shouldn't he search for it? Why shouldn't he comb the
countryside? He could do it on Sundays. In that way, it wouldn't interfere
with his work at all. He never knew what to do with his Sundays.

So Mr Boggis bought maps, large-scale maps of all the counties around
25 London, and with a fine pen he divided each of them up into a series of
squares. Each of these squares covered an actual area of five miles by five,
which was about as much territory, he estimated, as he could cope with on
a single Sunday, were he to comb it thoroughly. He didn't want the towns
and the villages. It was the comparatively isolated places, the large
30 farmhouses and the rather dilapidated country mansions, that he was
looking for; and in this way, if he did one square each Sunday, fifty-two
squares a year, he would gradually cover every farm and every country
house in the Home Counties.

But obviously there was a bit more to it than that. Country folk are a
35 suspicious lot. So are the impoverished rich. You can't go about ringing
their bells and expecting them to show you around their houses just for
the asking, because they won't do it. That wasy you would never get
beyond the front door. How then was he to gain admittance? Perhaps it
would be best if he didn't let them know he was a dealer at all. He could be

the telephone man, the plumber, the gas inspector. He could even be a clergymean. . . .

From this point on, the whole scheme began to take on a more practical aspect. Mr Boggis ordered a large quantity of superior cards on which the
5   following legend was engraved:

THE REVEREND

CYRIL WINNINGTON BOGGIS

President of the Society	In association with
for the Preservation of	The Victoria and
Rare Furniture	Albert Museum

From now on, every Sunday, he was going to be a nice old parson spending his holiday travelling around on a labour of love for the
15   'Society', compiling an inventory of the treasures that lay hidden in the country homes of England. And who in the world was going to kick him out when they heard that one?

Nobody.

And then, once he was inside, if he happened to spot something he
20   really wanted, well – he knew a hundred different ways of dealing with that.

Rather to Mr Boggis's surprise, the scheme worked. In fact, the friendliness with which he was received in one house after another through the countryside was, in the beginning, quite embarrassing, even
25   to him. A slice of cold pie, a glass of port, a cup of tea, a basket of plums, even a full sit-down Sunday dinner with the family, such things were constantly being pressed upon him. Sooner or later, of course, there had been some bad moments and a number of unpleasant incidents, but then nine years is more than four hundred Sundays, and that adds up to a great
30   quantity of houses visited. All in all, it had been an interesting, exciting and lucrative business.

And now it was another Sunday and Mr Boggis was operating in the county of Buckinghamshire, in one of the most northerly squares on his map, about ten miles from Oxford, and as he drove down the hill and
35   headed for his first house, the dilapidated Queen Anne, he began to get the feeling that this was going to be one of his lucky days.

He parked the car about a hundred yards from the gates and got out to walk the rest of the way. He never liked people to see his car until after a deal was completed. A dear old clergyman and a large station-wagon somehow never seemed quite right together. Also the short walk gave him time to examine the property closely from the outside and to assume the mood most likely to be suitable for the occasion.

Mr Boggis strode briskly up the drive. He was a small fat-legged man
5　with a belly. The face was round and rosy, quite perfect for the part, and the two large brown eyes that bulged out at you from this rosy face gave an impression of gentle imbecility. He was dressed in a black suit with the usual parson's dog-collar round his neck, and on his head a soft black hat. He carried an old oak walking-stick which lent him, in his opinion, a
10　rather rustic easy-going air.

He approached the front door and rang the bell. He heard the sound of footsteps in the hall and the door opened and suddenly there stood before him, or rather above him, a gigantic woman dressed in riding-breeches. Even through the smoke of her cigarette he could smell the powerful
15　odour of stables and horse manure that clung about her.

'Yes?' she asked, looking at him suspiciously. 'What is it you want?'

Mr Boggis, who half expected her to whinny any moment, raised his hat, made a little bow, and handed her his card. 'I do apologize for bothering you,' he said, and then he waited, watching her face as she read
20　the message.

'I don't understand,' she said, handing back the card, 'What is it you want?'

Mr Boggis explained about the Society for the Preservation of Rare Furniture.
25　'This wouldn't by any chance be something to do with the Socialist Party?' she asked, staring at him fiercely from under a pair of pale bushy brows.

From then on, it was easy. A Tory in riding-breeches, male or female, was always a sitting duck for Mr Boggis. He spent two minutes delivering
30　an impassioned eulogy on the extreme Right Wing of the Conservative Party, then two more denouncing the Socialists. As a clincher, he made particular reference to the Bill that the Socialists had once introduced for the abolition of blood-sports in the country, and went on to inform his listener that his idea of heaven – 'though you better not tell the bishop, my
35　dear' – was a place where one could hunt the fox, the stag, and the hare with large packs of tireless hounds from morn till night every day of the week, including Sundays.

Watching her as he spoke, he could see the magic beginning to do its work. The woman was grinning now, showing Mr Boggis a set of enormous, slightly yellow teeth. 'Madam,' he cried, 'I beg of you, *please* don't get me started on Socialism.' At that point, she let out a great guffaw of laughter, raised an enormous red hand, and slapped him so hard on the shoulder that he nearly went over.

5   'Come in!' she shouted. 'I don't know what the hell you want, but come on in!'

Unfortunately, and rather surprisingly, there was nothing of any value in the whole house, and Mr Boggis, who never wasted time on barren territory, soon made his excuses and took his leave. The whole visit had
10   taken less than fifteen minutes, and that, he told himself as he climbed back into his car and started off for the next place, was exactly as it should be.

From now on, it was all farmhouses, and the nearest was about half a mile up the road. It was a large half-timbered brick building of
15   considerable age, and there was a magnificent pear tree still in blossom covering almost the whole of the south wall.

Mr Boggis knocked on the door. He waited, but no one came. He knocked again, but still there was no answer, so he wandered around the back to look for the farmer among the cowsheds. There was no one there
20   either. He guessed that they must all still be in church, so he began peering in the windows to see if he could spot anything interesting. There was nothing in the dining-room. Nothing in the library either. He tried the next window, the living-room, and there, right under his nose, in the little alcove that the window made, he saw a beautiful thing, a semi-circular
25   card-table in mahogany, richly veneered, and in the style of Hepplewhite, built around 1780.

'Ah-ha,' he said aloud, pressing his face hard against glass. 'Well done, Boggis.'

But that was not all. There was a chair there as well, a single chair, and if
30   he were not mistaken it was of an even finer quality than the table. Another Hepplewhite, wasn't it? And oh, what a beauty! The lattices on the back were finely carved with the honeysuckle, the husk, and the paterae, the caning on the seat was original, the legs were very gracefully turned and the two back ones had that peculiar outward splay that meant
35   so much. It was an exquisite chair. 'Before this day is done,' Mr Boggis said softly, 'I shall have the pleasure of sitting down upon that lovely seat.' He never bought a chair without doing this. It was a favourite test of his, and it was always an intriguing sight to see him lowering himself delicately into the seat, waiting for the 'give', expertly gauging the precise but

infinitesimal degree of shrinkage that the years had caused in the mortice and dovetail joints.

But there was no hurry, he told himself. He would return here later. He had the whole afternoon before him.

The next farm was situated some way back in the fields, and in order to keep his car out of sight, Mr Boggis had to leave it on the road and walk about six hundred yards along a straight track that led directly into the back yard of the farmhouse. This place, he noticed as he approached, was a good deal smaller than the last, and he didn't hold out much hope for it. It looked rambling and dirty, and some of the sheds were clearly in bad repair.

There were three men standing in a close group in a corner of the yard, and one of them had two large black greyhounds with him, on leashes. When the men caught sight of Mr Boggis walking forward in his black suit and parson's collar, they stopped talking and seemed suddenly to stiffen and freeze, becoming absolutely still, motionless, three faces turned towards him, watching him suspiciously as he approached.

The oldest of the three was a stumpy man with a wide frog mouth and small shifty eyes, and although Mr Boggis didn't know it, his name was Rummins and he was the owner of the farm.

The tall youth beside him, who appeared to have something wrong with one eye, was Bert, the son of Rummins.

The shortish flat-faced man with a narrow corrugated brow and immensely broad shoulders was Claud. Claud had dropped in on Rummins in the hope of getting a piece of pork or ham out of him from the pig that had been killed the day before. Claud knew about the killing – the noise of it had carried far across the fields – and he also knew that a man should have a government permit to do that sort of thing, and that Rummins didn't have one.

'Good afternoon,' Mr Boggis said. 'Isn't it a lovely day?'

None of the three men moved. At that moment they were all thinking precisely the same thing – that somehow or other this clergyman, who was certainly not the local fellow, had been sent to poke his nose into their business and to report what he found to the government.

'What beautiful dogs,' Mr Boggis said. 'I must say I've never been greyhound-racing myself, but they tell me it's a fascinating sport.'

Again the silence, and Mr Boggis glanced quickly from Rummins to Bert, then to Claud, then back again to Rummins, and he noticed that each of them had the same peculiar expression on his face, something between a jeer and a challenge, with a contemptuous curl to the mouth and a sneer around the nose.

'Might I inquire if you are the owner?' Mr Boggis asked, undaunted, addressing himself to Rummins.

5 'What is it you want?'

'I do apologize for troubling you, especially on a Sunday.'

Mr Boggis offered his card and Rummins took it and held it up close to his face. The other two didn't move, but their eyes swivelled over to one side, trying to see.

10 'And what exactly might you be wanting?' Rummins asked.

For the second time that morning, Mr Boggis explained at some length the aims and ideals of the Society for the Preservation of Rare Furniture.

'We don't have any,' Rummins told him when it was over. 'You're wasting your time.'

15 'Now, just a minute, sir,' Mr Boggis said, raising a finger. 'The last man who said that to me was an old farmer down in Sussex, and when he finally let me into his house, d'you know what I found? A dirty-looking old chair in the corner of the kitchen, and it turned out to be worth *four hundred pounds*! I showed him how to sell it, and he bought himself a new tractor

20 with the money.'

'What on earth are you talking about?' Claud said. 'There ain't no chair in the world worth four hundred pound.'

'Excuse me,' Mr Boggis answered primly, 'but there are plenty of chairs in England worth more than twice that figure. And you know where they

25 are? They're tucked away in the farms and cottages all over the country, with the owners using them as steps and ladders and standing on them with hobnailed boots to reach a pot of jam out of the top cupboard or to hang a picture. This is the truth I'm telling you, my friends.'

Rummins shifted uneasily on his feet. 'You mean to say all you want to

30 do is go inside and stand there in the middle of the room and look around?'

'Exactly,' Mr Boggis said. He was at last beginning to sense what the trouble might be. 'I don't want to pry into your cupboards or into your larder. I just want to look at the furniture to see if you happen to have any

35 treasures here, and then I can write about them in our Society magazine.'

'You know what I think?' Rummins said, fixing him with his small wicked eyes. 'I think you're after buying the stuff yourself. Why else would you be going to all this trouble?'

'Oh, dear me. I only wish I had the money. Of course, if I saw something that I took a great fancy to, and it wasn't beyond my means, I might be tempted to make an offer. But alas, that rarely happens.'

'Well,' Rummins said, 'I don't suppose there's any harm in your taking a look around if that's all you want.' He led the way across the yard to the back door of the farmhouse, and Mr Boggis followed him; so did the son Bert, and Claud with his two dogs. They went through the kitchen, where the only furniture was a cheap deal table with a dead chicken lying on it, and they emerged into a fairly large, exceedingly filthy living-room.

And there it was! Mr Boggis saw it at once, and he stopped dead in his tracks and gave a little shrill gasp of shock. Then he stood there for five, ten, fifteen seconds at least, staring like an idiot, unable to believe, not daring to believe what he saw before him. It *couldn't* be true, not possibly! But the longer he stared, the more true it began to seem. After all, there it was standing against the wall right in front of him, as real and as solid as the house itself. And who in the world could possibly make a mistake about a thing like that? Admittedly it was painted white, but that made not the slightest difference. Some idiot had done that. The paint could easily be stripped off. But good God! Just look at it! And in a place like this!

At this point, Mr Boggis became aware of the three men, Rummins, Bert and Claud, standing together in a group over by the fireplace, watching him intently. They had seen him stop and gasp and stare, and they must have seen his face turning red, or maybe it was white, but in any event they had seen enough to spoil the whole goddamn business if he didn't do something about it quick. In a flash, Mr Boggis clapped one hand over his heart, staggered to the nearest chair, and collapsed into it, breathing heavily.

'What's the matter with you?' Claud asked.

'It's nothing,' he gasped. 'I'll be all right in a minute. Please – a glass of water. It's my heart.'

Bert fetched him the water, handed it to him, and stayed close beside him, staring down at him with a fatuous leer on his face.

'I thought maybe you were looking at something,' Rummins said. The wide frog-mouth widened a fraction further into a crafty grin, showing the stubs of several broken teeth.

'No, no,' Mr Boggis said. 'Oh dear me, no. It's just my heart. I'm so sorry. It happens every now and then. But it goes away quite quickly. I'll be all right in a couple of minutes.'

He *must* have time to think, he told himself. More important still, he

must have time to compose himself thoroughly before he said another word. Take it gently, Boggis. And whatever you do, keep calm. These people may be ignorant, but they are not stupid. They are suspicious and wary and sly. And if it is really true – no it *can't* be, it *can't* be
5 true. . . .

He was holding one hand up over his eyes in a gesture of pain, and now, very carefully, secretly, he made a little crack between two of the fingers and peeked through.

Sure enough, the thing was still there, and on this occasion he took a
10 good long look at it. Yes – he had been right the first time! There wasn't the slightest doubt about it! It was really unbelievable!

What he saw was a piece of furniture that any expert would have given almost anything to acquire. To a layman, it might not have appeared particularly impressive, especially when covered over as it was with dirty
15 white paint, but to Mr Boggis it was a dealer's dream. He knew, as does every other dealer in Europe and America, that among the most celebrated and coveted examples of eighteenth-century English furniture in existence are the three famous pieces known as 'The Chippendale Commodes'. He knew their history backwards – that the first was
20 'discovered' in 1920, in a house at Moreton-in-Marsh, and was sold at Sotheby's the same year; that the other two turned up in the same auction rooms a year later, both coming out of Raynham Hall, Norfolk. They all fetched enormous prices. He couldn't quite remember the exact figure for the first one, or even the second, but he knew for certain that the last one
25 to be sold had fetched thirty-nine hundred guineas. And that was in 1921! Today the same piece would surely be worth ten thousand pounds. Some man, Mr Boggis couldn't remember his name, had made a study of these commodes fairly recently and had proved that all three must have come from the same workshop, for the veneers were all from the same log, and
30 the same set of templates had been used in the construction of each. No invoices had been found for any of them, but all the experts were agreed that these three commodes could have been executed only by Thomas Chippendale himself, with his own hands, at the most exalted period in his career.

35 And here, Mr Boggis kept telling himself as he peered cautiously through the crack in his fingers, here was the fourth Chippendale Commode! And *he* had found it! He would be rich! He would also be famous! Each of the other three was known throughout the furniture world by a special name – The Chastleton Commode, The First Raynham

Commode, The Second Raynham Commode. This one would go down in history as The Boggis Commode! Just imagine the faces of the boys up there in London when they got a look at it tomorrow morning! And the luscious offers coming in from the big fellows over in the West End – Frank Partridge, Mallett, Jetley, and the rest of them! There would be a picture of it in *The Times*, and it would say, 'The very fine Chippendale Commode which was recently discovered by Mr Cyril Boggis, a London Dealer. . . .' Dear God, what a stir he was going to make!

This one here, Mr Boggis thought, was almost exactly similar to the Second Raynham Commode. (All three, the Chastleton and the two Raynhams, differed from one another in a number of small ways). It was a most impressive handsome affair, built in the French rococo style of Chippendale's Directoire period, a kind of large fat chest-of-drawers set upon four carved and fluted legs that raised it about a foot from the ground. There were six drawers in all, two long ones in the middle and two shorter ones on either side. The serpentine front was magnificently ornamented along the top and sides and bottom, and also vertically between each set of drawers, with intricate carvings of festoons and scrolls and clusters. The brass handles, although partly obscured by white paint, appeared to be superb. It was, of course, a rather 'heavy' piece, but the design had been executed with such elegance and grace that the heaviness was in no way offensive.

'How're you feeling now?' Mr Boggis heard someone saying.

'Thank you, thank you, I'm much better already. It passes quickly. My doctor says it's nothing to worry about really so long as I rest for a few minutes whenever it happens. Ah yes,' he said, raising himself slowly to his feet. 'That's better. I'm all right now.'

A trifle unsteadily, he began to move around the room examining the furniture, one piece at a time, commenting upon it briefly. He could see at once that apart from the commode it was a very poor lot.

'Nice oak table,' he said. 'But I'm afraid it's not old enough to be of any interest. Good comfortable chairs, but quite modern, yes, quite modern. Now this cupboard, well, it's rather attractive, but again, not valuable. This chest-of-drawers' – he walked casually past the Chippendale Commode and gave it a little contemptuous flip with his fingers – 'worth a few pounds, I dare say, but no more. A rather crude reproduction, I'm afraid. Probably made in Victorian times. Did you paint it white?'

'Yes,' Rummins said, 'Bert did it.'

'A very wise move. It's considerably less offensive in white.'

'That's a strong piece of furniture,' Rummins said, 'Some nice carving on it too.'

'Machine-carved,' Mr Boggis answered superbly, bending down to examine the exquisite craftsmanship. 'You can tell it a mile off. But still, I suppose it's quite pretty in its way. It has its points.'

He began to saunter off, then he checked himself and turned slowly back again. He placed the tip of one finger against the point of his chin, laid his head over to one side, and frowned as though deep in thought.

'You know what?' he said, looking at the commode, speaking so casually that his voice kept trailing off. 'I've just remembered . . . I've been wanting a set of legs something like that for a long time. I've got a rather curious table in my own little home, one of those low things that people put in front of the sofa, sort of a coffee-table, and last Michaelmas, when I moved house, the foolish movers damaged the legs in the most shocking way. I'm very fond of that table. I always keep my big Bible on it, and all my sermon notes.'

He paused, stroking his chin with the finger. 'Now I was just thinking. These legs on your chest-of-drawers might be very suitable. Yes, they might indeed. They could easily be cut off and fixed on to my table.'

He looked around and saw the three men standing absolutely still, watching him suspiciously, three pairs of eyes, all different but equally mistrusting, small pig-eyes for Rummins, large slow eyes for Claud, and two odd eyes for Bert, one of them very queer and boiled and misty pale, with a little black dot in the centre, like a fish eye on a plate.

Mr Boggis smiled and shook his head. 'Come, come, what on earth am I saying? I'm talking as though I owned the piece myself. I do apologize.'

'What you mean to say is you'd like to buy it,' Rummins said.

'Well . . .' Mr Boggis glanced back at the commode, frowning. 'I'm not sure. I might . . . and then again . . . on second thoughts . . . no . . . I think it might be a bit too much trouble. It's not worth it. I'd better leave it.'

'How much were you thinking of offering?' Rummins asked.

'Not much, I'm afraid. You see, this is not a genuine antique. It's merely a reproduction.'

'I'm not so sure about that,' Rummins told him. 'It's been in *here* over twenty years, and before that it was up at the Manor House. I bought it there myself at auction when the old Squire died. You can't tell me that thing's new.'

'It's not exactly new, but it's certainly not more than about sixty years old.'

158

'It's more than that,' Rummins said. 'Bert, where's that bit of paper you once found at the back of one of them drawers? That old bill.'

The boy looked vacantly at his father.

Mr Boggis opened his mouth, then quickly shut it again without uttering a sound. He was beginning literally to shake with excitement, and to calm himself he walked over to the window and stared out at a plump brown hen pecking around for stray grains of corn in the yard.

'It was in the back of that drawer underneath all them rabbit snares,' Rummins was saying. 'Go on and fetch it out and show it to the parson.'

When Bert went forward to the commode, Mr Boggis turned round again. He couldn't stand not watching him. He saw him pull out one of the big middle drawers, and he noticed the beautiful way in which the drawer slid open. He saw Bert's hand dipping inside and rummaging around among a lot of wires and strings.

'You mean this?' Bert lifted out a piece of folded yellowing paper and carried it over to the father, who unfolded it and held it up close to his face.

'You can't tell me this writing ain't bloody old,' Rummins said, and he held the paper out to Mr Boggis, whose whole arm was shaking as he took it. It was brittle and it crackled slightly between his fingers. The writing was in a long sloping copperplate hand:

Edward Montague, Esq.   Dr
                                          To Thos. Chippendale
A large mahogany Commode Table of exceeding fine wood, very rich carvd, set upon fluted legs, two very neat shapd long drawers in the middle part and two ditto on each side, with rich chasd Brass Handles and Ornaments, the whole completely finished in the most exquisite taste £87

Mr Boggis was holding on to himself tight and fighting to suppress the excitement that was spinning round inside him and making him dizzy. Oh God, it was wonderful! With the invoice, the value had climbed even higher. What in heaven's name would it fetch now? Twelve thousand pounds? Fourteen? Maybe fifteen or even twenty? Who knows?

Oh, boy!

He tossed the paper contemptuously on to the table and said quietly, 'It's exactly what I told you, a Victorian reproduction. This is simply the invoice the seller – the man who made it and passed it off as an antique – gave to his client. I've seen lots of them. You'll notice that he doesn't say he made it himself. That would give the game away.'

'Say what you like,' Rummins announced, 'but that's an old piece of paper.'

5 'Of course it is, my dear friend. It's Victorian, late Victorian. About eighteen ninety. Sixty or seventy years old. I've seen hundreds of them. That was a time when masses of cabinet makers did nothing else but apply themselves to faking the fine furniture of the century before.'

'Listen, Parson,' Rummins said, pointing at him with a thick dirty
10 finger, 'I'm not saying as how you may not know a fair bit about this furniture business, but what I *am* saying is this: How on earth can you be so mighty sure it's a fake when you haven't even seen what it looks like underneath all that paint?'

'Come here,' Mr Boggis said. 'Come over here and I'll show you.' He
15 stood beside the commode and waited for them to gather round. 'Now, anyone got a knife?'

Claud produced a horn-handled pocket knife, and Mr Boggis took it and opened the smallest blade. Then, working with apparent casualness but actually with extreme care, he began chipping off the white paint from
20 a small area on the top of the commode. The paint flaked away cleanly from the old hard varnish underneath, and when he had cleared away about three square inches, he stepped back and said, 'Now, take a look at that!'

It was beautiful – warm little patch of mahogany, glowing like a topaz,
25 rich and dark with the true colour of its two hundred years.

'What's wrong with it?' Rummins asked.

'It's processed! Anyone can see that!'

'How can you see it, Mister? You tell us.'

'Well, I must say that's a trifle difficult to explain. It's chiefly a matter of
30 experience. My experience tells me that without the slightest doubt this wood has been processed with lime. That's what they use for mahogany, to give it that dark aged colour. For oak, they use potash salts, and for walnut it's nitric acid, but for mahogany it's always lime.'

The three men moved a little closer to peer at the wood. There was a
35 slight stirring of interest among them now. It was always intriguing to hear about some new form of crookery or deception.

'Look closely at the grain. You see that touch of orange in among the dark red-brown. That's the sign of lime.'

They leaned forward, their noses close to the wood, first Rummins, then Claud, then Bert.

'And then there's the patina,' Mr Boggis continued.

'The what?'

He explained to them the meaning of this word as applied to furniture.

'My dear friends, you've no idea the trouble these rascals will go to to imitate the hard beautiful bronze-like appearance of genuine patina. It's terrible, really terrible, and it makes me quite sick to speak of it!' He was spitting each word sharply off the tip of the tongue and making a sour mouth to show his extreme distaste. The men waited, hoping for more secrets.

'The time and trouble that some mortals will go to in order to deceive the innocent!' Mr Boggis cried. 'It's perfectly disgusting! D'you know what they did here, my friends? I can recognize it clearly. I can almost *see* them doing it, the long, complicated ritual of rubbing the wood with linseed oil, coating it over with french polish that has been cunningly coloured, brushing it down with pumice-stone and oil, bees-waxing it with a wax that contains dirt and dust, and finally giving it the heat treatment to crack the polish so that it looks like two-hundred-year-old varnish! It really upsets me to contemplate such knavery!'

The three men continued to gaze at the little patch of dark wood.

'Feel it!' Mr Boggis ordered. 'Put your fingers on it! There, how does it feel, warm or cold?'

'Feels cold,' Rummins said.

'Exactly, my friend! It happens to be a fact that faked patina is always cold to the touch. Real patina has a curiously warm feel to it.'

'This feels normal,' Rummins said, ready to argue.

'No, sir, it's cold. But of course it takes an experienced and sensitive finger-tip to pass a positive judgement. You couldn't really be expected to judge this any more than I could be expected to judge the quality of your barley. Everything in life, my dear sir, is experience.'

The men were staring at this queer moon-faced clergyman with the bulging eyes, not quite so suspiciously now because he did seem to know a bit about his subject. But they were still a long way from trusting him.

Mr Boggis bent down and pointed to one of the metal drawer handles on the commode. 'This is another place where the fakers go to work,' he said. 'Old brass normally has a colour and character all of its own. Did you know that?'

They stared at him, hoping for still more secrets.

'But the trouble is that they've become exceedingly skilled at matching it. In fact it's almost impossible to tell the difference between "genuine old" and "faked old". I don't mind admitting that it has me guessing. So there's not really any point in our scraping the paint off these handles. We wouldn't be any the wiser.'

5   'How can you possibly make new brass look like old?' Claud said. 'Brass doesn't rust, you know.'

'You are quite right, my friend. But these scoundrels have their own secret methods.'

'Such as what?' Claud asked. Any information of this nature was
10 valuable, in his opinion. One never knew when it might come in handy.

'All they have to do,' Mr Boggis said, 'is to place these handles overnight in a box of mahogany shavings saturated in sal ammoniac. The sal ammoniac turns the metal green, but if you rub off the green, you will find underneath it a fine soft silvery-warm lustre, a lustre identical to that
15 which comes with very old brass. Oh, it is so bestial, the things they do! With iron they have another trick.'

'What do they do with iron?' Claud asked, fascinated.

'Iron's easy,' Mr Boggis said. 'Iron locks and plates and hinges are simply buried in common salt and they come out all rusted and pitted in
20 no time.'

'All right,' Rummins said. 'So you admit you can't tell about the handles. For all you know, they may be hundreds and hundreds of years old. Correct?'

'Ah', Mr Boggis whispered, fixing Rummins with two big bulging
25 brown eyes. 'That's where you're wrong. Watch this.'

From his jacket pocket, he took out a small screwdriver. At the same time, although none of them saw him do it, he also took out a little brass screw which he kept well hidden in the palm of his hand. Then he selected one of the screws in the commode – there were four to each handle – and
30 began carefully scraping all trace of white paint from its head. When he had done this, he started slowly to unscrew it.

'If this is a genuine old brass screw from the eighteenth century,' he was saying, 'the spiral will be slightly uneven and you'll be able to see quite easily that it has been hand-cut with a file. But if this brasswork is faked
35 from more recent times, Victorian or later, then obviously the screw will be of the same period. It will be a mass-produced, machine-made article. Anyone can recognize a machine-made screw. Well, we shall see.'

It was not difficult, as he put his hands over the old screw and drew it out, for Mr Boggis to substitute the new one hidden in his palm. This was

162

another little trick of his, and through the years it had proved a most rewarding one. The pockets of his clergyman's jacket were always stocked with a quantity of cheap brass screws of various sizes.

'There you are,' he said, handing the modern screw to Rummins. 'Take a look at that. Notice the exact evenness of the spiral? See it? Of course you do. It's just a cheap common little screw you yourself could buy today in any ironmonger's in the country.'

The screw was handed round from the one to the other, each examining it carefully. Even Rummins was impressed now.

Mr Boggis put the screwdriver back in his pocket together with the fine hand-cut screw that he'd taken from the commode, and then he turned and walked slowly past the three men towards the door.

'My dear friends,' he said, pausing at the entrance to the kitchen, 'it was so good of you to let me peep inside your little home – so kind. I do hope I haven't been a terrible old bore.'

Rummins glanced up from examining the screw. 'You didn't tell us what you were going to offer,' he said.

'Ah,' Mr Boggis said. 'That's quite right. I didn't, did I? Well, to tell you the honest truth, I think it's all a bit too much trouble. I think I'll leave it.'

'How much would you give?'

'You mean that you really wish to part with it?'

'I didn't say I wished to part with it. I asked you how much.'

Mr Boggis looked across at the commode, and he laid his head first to one side, then to the other, and he frowned, and pushed out his lips, and shrugged his shoulders, and gave a little scornful wave of the hand as though to say the thing was hardly worth thinking about really, was it?

'Shall we say . . . ten pounds. I think that would be fair.'

'Ten pounds!' Rummins cried. 'Don't be so ridiculous, Parson, *please*!'

'It's worth more'n that for firewood!' Claud said, disgusted.

'Look here at the bill!' Rummins went on, stabbing that precious document so fiercely with his dirty fore-finger that Mr Boggis became alarmed. 'It tells you exactly what it cost! Eighty-seven pounds! And that's when it was new. Now it's antique it's worth double!'

'If you'll pardon me, no, sir, it's not. It's a second-hand reproduction. But I'll tell you what, my friend – I'm being rather reckless, I can't help it – I'll go up as high as fifteen pounds. How's that?'

'Make it fifty,' Rummins said.

A delicious little quiver like needles ran all the way down the back of Mr Boggis's legs and then under the soles of his feet. He had it now. It was his. No question about that. But the habit of buying cheap, as cheap as it was humanly possible to buy, acquired by years of necessity and practice, was too strong in him now to permit him to give in so easily.

'My dear man,' he whispered softly, 'I only *want* the legs. Possibly I
5 could find some use for the drawers later on, but the rest of it, the carcass itself, as your friend so rightly said, it's firewood, that's all.'

'Make it thirty-five,' Rummins said.

'I *couldn't* sir, I *couldn't*! It's not worth it. And I simply mustn't allow myself to haggle like this about a price. It's all wrong. I'll make you one
10 final offer, and then I must go. Twenty pounds.'

'I'll take it,' Rummins snapped. 'It's yours.'

'Oh dear,' Mr Boggis said, clasping his hands. 'There I go again. I should never have started this in the first place.'

'You can't back out now, Parson. A deal's a deal.'
15 'Yes, yes, I know.'

'How're you going to take it?'

'Well, let me see. Perhaps if I were to drive my car up into the yard, you gentlemen would be kind enough to help me load it?'

'In a car? This thing'll never go in a car! You'll need a truck for this!'
20 'I don't think so. Anyway, we'll see. My car's on the road. I'll be back in a jiffy. We'll manage it somehow, I'm sure.'

Mr Boggis walked out into the yard and through the gate and then down the long track that led across the field towards the road. He found himself giggling quite uncontrollably, and there was a feeling inside him
25 as though hundreds and hundreds of tiny bubbles were rising up from his stomach and bursting merrily in the top of his head, like sparkling-water. All the buttercups in the field were suddenly turning into golden sovereigns, glistening in the sunlight. The ground was littered with them, and he swung off the track on to the grass so that he could walk among
30 them and tread on them and hear the little metallic tinkle they made as he kicked them around with his toes. He was finding it difficult to stop himself from breaking into a run. But clergymen never run; they walk slowly. Walk slowly, Boggis. Keep calm, Boggis. There's no hurry now. The commode is yours! Yours for twenty pounds, and it's worth fifteen or
35 twenty thousand! The Boggis Commode! In ten minutes it'll be loaded into your car – it'll go in easily – and you'll be driving back to London and singing all the way! Mr Boggis driving the Boggis Commode home in the Boggis car. Historic occasion. What *wouldn't* a newspaperman give to get a picture of that! Should he arrange it? Perhaps

he should. Wait and see. Oh, glorious day! Oh, lovely sunny summer day! Oh, glory be!

Back in the farmhouse, Rummins was saying, 'Fancy that old bastard giving twenty pounds for a load of junk like this.'

'You did very nicely, Mr Rummins,' Claud told him. 'You think he'll pay you?'

'We don't put it in the car till he do.'

'And what if it won't go in the car?' Claud asked. 'You know what I think, Mr Rummins? You want my honest opinion? I think the bloody thing's too big to go in the car. And then what happens? Then he's going to say to hell with it and just drive off without it and you'll never see him again. Nor the money either. He didn't seem all that keen on having it, you know.'

Rummins paused to consider this new and rather alarming prospect.

'How can a thing like that possibly go in a car?' Claud went on relentlessly. 'A parson never has a big car anyway. You ever seen a parson with a big car, Mr Rummins?'

'Can't say I have.'

'Exactly! And now listen to me. I've got an idea. He told us, didn't he, that it was only the legs he was wanting. Right? So all we've got to do is to cut 'em off quick right here on the spot before he comes back, then it'll be sure to go in the car. All we're doing is saving him the trouble of cutting them off himself when he gets home. How about it, Mr Rummins?' Claud's flat bovine face glimmered with a mawkish pride.

'It's not such a bad idea at that,' Rummins said, looking at the commode. 'In fact it's a bloody good idea. Come on then, we'll have to hurry. You and Bert carry it out into the yard. I'll get the saw. Take the drawers out first.'

Within a couple of minutes, Claud and Bert had carried the commode outside and had laid it upside down in the yard amidst the chicken droppings and cow dung and mud. In the distance, half-way across the field, they could see a small figure striding along the path towards the road. They paused to watch. There was something rather comical about the way in which this figure was conducting itself. Every now and again it would break into a trot, then it did a kind of hop, skip and jump, and once it seemed as though the sound of a cheerful song came rippling faintly to them from across the meadow.

'I reckon he's barmy,' Claud said, and Bert grinned darkly, rolling his misty eye slowly round in its socket.

Rummins came waddling over from the shed, squat and froglike, carrying a long saw. Claud took the saw away from him and went to work.

'Cut 'em close,' Rummins said. 'Don't forget he's going to use 'em on another table.'

5   The mahogany was hard and very dry, and as Claud worked, a fine red dust sprayed out from the edge of the saw and fell softly to the ground. One by one, the legs came off, and when they were all severed, Bert stooped down and arranged them carefully in a row.

Claud stepped back to survey the results of his labour. There was a
10 longish pause.

'Just let me ask you one question, Mr Rummins,' he said slowly. 'Even now, could *you* put that enormous thing into the back of a car?'

'Not unless it was a van.'

'Correct!' Claud cried. 'And parsons don't have vans, you know. All
15 they've got usually is piddling little Morris Eights or Austin Sevens.'

'The legs is all he wants,' Rummins said. 'If the rest of it won't go in, then he can leave it. He can't complain. He's got the legs.'

'Now you know better'n that, Mr Rummins,' Claud said patiently. 'You know damn well he's going to start knocking the price if he don't get every
20 single bit of this into the car. A parson's just as cunning as the rest of 'em when it comes to money, don't you make any mistake about that. Especially this old boy. So why don't we give him his firewood now and be done with it. Where d'you keep the axe?

'I reckon that's fair enough,' Rummins said. 'Bert, go fetch the axe.'
25 Bert went into the shed and fetched a tall woodcutter's axe and gave it to Claud. Claud spat on the palms of his hands and rubbed them together. Then, with a long-armed high-swinging action, he began fiercely attacking the legless carcass of the commode.

It was hard work, and it took several minutes before he had the whole
30 thing more or less smashed to pieces.

'I'll tell you one thing,' he said, straightening up, wiping his brow. 'That was a bloody good carpenter put this job together and I don't care what the parson says.'

'We're just in time!' Rummins called out. 'Here he comes!'

Questions

The Author

Roald Dahl (1916–1990) was born in South Wales of Norwegian parents. He joined the RAF during the Second World War and his first collection of short stories, *Over to You* (1946), deals with flying. Other collections are *Kiss Kiss* (1959), from which this story is taken and *Tales of the Unexpected* (1979), which became a popular television series. Dahl also wrote many children's stories, including *James and the Giant Peach* (1961).

The Story

Mr Boggis is a very clever man in the antique furniture business. He travels round the country buying up antiques at a very low price, and is really doing very well for himself. One day, however, he meets some people who are as clever as he is, in a different way!

Written Work

In this story there are many descriptions of furniture. Give a detailed description of a piece of furniture in your own home.

Discussion

1 Describe Mr Boggis. What does he look like? What is his character like?
2 How does he set about the task of finding antiques?
3 Who is the first person Mr Boggis meets on Sunday in Buckinghamshire? How does he get her to like him?
4 Why are the three men with the greyhounds suspicious of Mr Boggis? What are they trying to hide?
5 Describe Mr Boggis's reaction when he goes into the living-room and sees the commode.
6 How does he make the men think that the commode is a fake?
7 What happens at the end of the story?
8 What seems to be the moral of the story?

Words and Phrases

I

explode: burst into flower. (146,5)

Queen Anne: style of building common during the time of Queen Anne (1665–1714). (146,22)

Chinese or Gothic period: the time when Thomas Chippendale (1717–1779) used Chinese or Gothic designs. (147,36)

Sevenoaks: town in county of Kent, south-east of London. (148,13)

gas inspector: man who comes round to find out how much gas a household has used in a certain period. (150,1)

the Victoria and Albert Museum: museum in Kensington, London. (150,9)

labour of love: unpaid work done for a good cause. (150,14)

dog-collar: straight high collar divided at back, usually worn by English clergymen. (151,8)

lend: give. (151,9)

Tory: member of the English Conservative political party. (151,28)

sitting duck: someone easy to deal with. (151,29)

blood-sports: sports in which animals are killed. (151,33)

make one's excuses: give one's reasons for having to leave. (152,9)

lattices: pieces of wood arranged in a criss-cross pattern. (152,31)

paterae: flat drinking bowls. (152,33)

Sotheby's: well-known London firm of auctioneers. (156,21)

luscious: very good. (157,4)

big fellows: (here) the important furniture dealers. (157,4)

Directoire: period in French history (1795–1799). (157,13)

carvd: carved. (159,25)

chasd: chased; with design cut into them. (159,26)

processed: treated in a special way to get a special effect. (160,31)

sal ammoniac: ammonium chloride. (162,13)

delicious: very pleasant. (163,38)

carcass: the main body of the commode. (164,5)

bastard: an impolite way of talking about a man. (165,3)

close: as high up as possible. (166,3)

Morris Eights or Austin Sevens: small English cars. (166,15)

job: piece of furniture. (166,32)